T0311601

Cambridge Elements

Elements in Politics and Society in Southeast Asia
edited by
Edward Aspinall
Australian National University
Meredith L. Weiss
University at Albany, SUNY

ORGANIZED LABOR IN SOUTHEAST ASIA

Teri L. Caraway
University of Minnesota

CAMBRIDGE
UNIVERSITY PRESS

CAMBRIDGE
UNIVERSITY PRESS

Shaftesbury Road, Cambridge CB2 8EA, United Kingdom

One Liberty Plaza, 20th Floor, New York, NY 10006, USA

477 Williamstown Road, Port Melbourne, VIC 3207, Australia

314–321, 3rd Floor, Plot 3, Splendor Forum, Jasola District Centre, New Delhi – 110025, India

103 Penang Road, #05–06/07, Visioncrest Commercial, Singapore 238467

Cambridge University Press is part of Cambridge University Press & Assessment, a department of the University of Cambridge.

We share the University's mission to contribute to society through the pursuit of education, learning and research at the highest international levels of excellence.

www.cambridge.org
Information on this title: www.cambridge.org/9781108722407

DOI: 10.1017/9781108630818

First published 2023

A catalogue record for this publication is available from the British Library.

ISBN 978-1-108-72240-7 Paperback
ISSN 2515-2998 (online)
ISSN 2515-298X (print)

Organized Labor in Southeast Asia

Elements in Politics and Society in Southeast Asia

DOI: 10.1017/9781108630818
First published online: January 2023

Teri L. Caraway
University of Minnesota

Author for correspondence: Teri L. Caraway, caraway@umn.edu

Abstract: This Element analyzes the economic and political forces behind the political marginalization of working-class organizations in Southeast Asia. It traces the roots of labor exclusion to the geopolitics of the early postwar period when many governments rolled back the left and established labor control regimes that prevented the re-emergence of working-class movements. This Element also examines the economic and political dynamics that perpetuated labor's containment in some countries and that produced a resurgence of labor mobilization in others in the twenty-first century. It also explains why democratization has had mixed effects on organized labor in Southeast Asia and analyzes three distinctive "anatomies of contention" of the region's feistiest labor movements in Cambodia, Indonesia, and Vietnam.

Keywords: labor, Southeast Asia, social movements, contentious politics, comparative politics

ISBNs: 9781108722407 (PB), 9781108630818 (OC)
ISSNs: 2515-2998 (online), 2515-298X (print)

Contents

1 Introduction

For much of the late twentieth century, organized labor was a silent presence in Southeast Asian politics. Despite rapid industrialization and a swelling proletariat in many countries in the region, working-class organizations were rarely serious players in national politics (Deyo 1989; Hadiz 1997; Hutchison and Brown 2001). Little surprise, then, that labor has not featured prominently in most analyses of Southeast Asian politics. To the extent that organized labor makes more than a passing appearance in scholarly narratives of the region's politics, they highlight its weakness, typically as a critical facilitating condition for export-oriented industrialization (Caraway 2007; Haggard 1990).

But organized labor was not always so peripheral to Southeast Asian politics (Deyo 1997; Hewison and Rodan 1994). Left-wing organizations and their associated trade unions were important actors in anti-colonial struggles, and in one case, Singapore, leftist unions nearly established a socialist government in the early 1960s (Deyo 1981; Hewison and Rodan 1994). As the region became embroiled in postwar geopolitical rivalries, however, the political climate became more fraught for both the left and working-class organizations (Hansson et al. 2020; Hewison and Rodan 1994). Regarded as avenues of communist infiltration, pro-Western governments in the region waged war on leftists and working class organizations (Deyo 1997). After rolling back the left, capitalist countries in Southeast Asia – Indonesia, Malaysia, the Philippines, Singapore, and Thailand – established regimes of labor control that checked labor mobilization for decades to come. Surviving working-class organizations were relatively docile, often under state control, organized a small proportion of the region's growing industrial workforce, and posed little threat to ruling elites. (Hewison and Rodan 1994).

In addition to geopolitics, the "lateness" of industrialization (Gerschenkron 1962) in Southeast Asia fostered less propitious conditions for the development of powerful labor movements. Industrialization only began in earnest after World War II, and capitalist countries initially promoted import-substituting industries, which absorbed little labor (Caraway 2007; Hewison 1997; Hutchison 1997; Rasiah 1997). In Latin America, import-substitution industrialization provided the material foundation for a populist coalition that incorporated labor (O'Donnell 1973), but in Southeast Asia, Cold War rivalries blocked this pathway. The higher capital intensity of late and dependent industrialization also resulted in a smaller industrial working class and a larger informal sector, creating a substantial reserve army of labor that structurally weakened the working class (Bellin 2002; Rueschemeyer et al. 1992).

As some countries in the region began to energetically turn their attention to expanding labor-intensive manufactured exports in the 1970s and 1980s, however, the industrial workforce grew rapidly, creating fertile conditions for a resurgence of working-class organizations (Caraway 2007; Hewison 1997; Hutchison 1997; Rasiah 1997; Rodan 1997). The labor control regimes established after the rollback of the left both prevented the re-emergence of militant unions and proved useful in assuring the low wages essential for export-oriented industrialization to succeed (Hadiz 1997; Kuruvilla 1996). Although significant episodes of working-class mobilization occurred in several countries – Thailand in the 1970s, the Philippines in the 1980s, and Indonesia in the 1990s – ruling elites soon squelched them, and by the turn of the century, there was little sign of industrial unrest.

The countries that ended up in the socialist camp – Cambodia, Laos, Myanmar, and Vietnam – followed a different pathway but with similar results. In Indochina, the devastation of the Vietnam War and poor economic performance in the years that followed stunted industrialization. In Burma as well, there was little industrial development because the military government pursued an idiosyncratic and isolationist economic policy (Than 2007). In all four countries, agricultural employment dwarfed that in industry. In addition to the small size of the working class, ruling parties in socialist states adopted forms of labor incorporation that limited the potential for trade unions to become vehicles for working-class mobilization. Communist parties in Laos and Vietnam – and in Cambodia after the fall of the Khmer Rouge – integrated a party-controlled union into their organizational structures, while in Burma the military regime eventually dissolved unions (Arnold and Campbell 2017; Fry 2008; Hansson 2003; Nuon and Serrano 2010).

In the twenty-first century, economic and political transformations disrupted or ruptured these postwar institutions of containment in some parts of Southeast Asia. Democratization in Indonesia and East Timor, political liberalization in Myanmar, and a surge of employment in labor-intensive export industries in Cambodia and Vietnam laid the groundwork for the re-emergence of worker mobilization. Although organized labor did not become a decisive political player at the national level in these countries, working-class contention became a prominent feature of political life and often prompted governments to make important concessions.

Labor contentiousness in Southeast Asia during the twenty-first century does not correlate with regime type or with conventional measures of labor strength such as union density or organizational concentration. This pattern of development affirms the findings of many comparative studies of labor politics that have found that democratization does not consistently herald a resurgence of labor movements (Caraway, Cook et al. 2015; Cook 2010; Crowley 2004; Crowley and Ost 2001; Evans and Sil 2020; Hutchison 2015; Ost 2005). In democracies, workers are freer to establish unions and, in most cases, also endure less state-sponsored violence. But this has not been enough to overcome other conditions that thwart organized labor in Southeast Asia. Although organized labor in some countries that democratized or liberalized became stronger – Indonesia, Myanmar, and Timor-Leste – in others organized labor has become weaker. Cambodia and Vietnam also illustrate that worker militancy can be greater in autocratic settings than in some democracies.

Organized Labor in Southeast Asia analyzes the development of organized labor since World War II. It offers insights into why the working class continues to be largely contained in some countries and feistier in others and grapples with the question of why democratization has had mixed effects on labor movements in the region. Section 2 traces the historical roots of labor containment in Southeast Asia to the geopolitics of the early postwar period, analyzing how countries aligned with the West rolled back leftist organizations and instituted systems of labor control that largely held workers in check during the twentieth century. With these historical legacies established, Section 3 brings the analysis to the twenty-first century, outlining the economic and political processes that have reproduced or disrupted these twentieth-century patterns. Section 4 analyzes the three countries where workers have proven to be the most contentious in the twenty-first century: Cambodia, Indonesia, and Vietnam. I develop a typology of patterns of labor contention and illustrate three distinctive "anatomies of contention." The concluding section summarizes the main findings and reflects on labor's response to the wave of autocratization that has swept through the region in recent years.

2 Postwar Legacies in the Twentieth Century

In the wake of Japan's defeat in World War II and amid the birth pangs of the Cold War, nationalist and anti-colonial movements in Southeast Asia rallied their forces to wrest independence from the western powers. Leftist organizations and their affiliated trade unions were central and sometimes dominant actors in these movements. Within two decades, however, governments allied with the West – Indonesia, Malaysia, the Philippines, Singapore, and Thailand – had stamped out the left and militant working-class organizations. With leftist groups defeated, governing elites established systems of labor control designed to prevent the resurrection of radical labor movements. Rollback and containment stuck. At the end of the century, unionization rates were low, and trade unions were hopelessly divided, defanged, or coopted by ruling parties.

Other countries in the region – Cambodia, Laos, Myanmar, and Vietnam – followed a distinctive pathway that nevertheless resulted in a strikingly similar outcome for organized labor. Western powers failed to roll back the left in these countries, but decades of war and economic closure took a heavy toll on the economy and society. Economies remained highly dependent on agriculture, and the industrial working class was small. In addition, the ruling parties either banned unions outright or subordinated them within party structures. Thus, at century's end, organized labor in socialist Southeast Asia bore many similarities to organized labor in capitalist Southeast Asia.

2.1 Rolling Back the Left and Containing Labor Movements in Capitalist Southeast Asia: Indonesia, Malaysia, the Philippines, Singapore, and Thailand

After Japan's defeat in 1945, the anti-colonial movements that gained strength during the war became a force to be reckoned with throughout the region. The tumult of the postwar period presented an opportunity, which the left seized. The "loss" of China in 1949 and the devastation of the Korean War in the early 1950s, however, placed Southeast Asia on the frontline of the global confrontation between communism and capitalism. Intent on staunching the spread of communism, the United States allied with conservative forces in the region to repress leftist organizations (Hansson et al. 2020; Hewison and Rodan 1994). By the mid-1950s, governments allied with the West had decimated the left in Malaysia, the Philippines, and Thailand, and by the mid-1960s in Indonesia and Singapore (see Table 1). With the defeat of the left, these capitalist and usually authoritarian regimes embarked on industrialization drives that structurally transformed their economies, sowing the seeds for the re-emergence of new, and potentially contentious, working-class movements. To avert this possibility, governments erected systems of labor control (see Table 1) that largely succeeded in keeping the working class under wraps.

2.1.1 Phase I: Rolling Back the Left

Leftist organizations and trade unions throughout Southeast Asia took full advantage of the political moment after the Japanese defeat in World War II to rally support for their cause. Among the groups that opposed the return of colonial forces, leftist organizations were influential and often dominant, and the working-class organizations aligned with them were usually the strongest. Many also had ties to the World Federation of Trade Unions (WFTU), established in 1945. Although the WFTU included both communist and noncommunist unions, western powers perceived it to be a Soviet front organization, and

Table 1 Rollback and labor control in capitalist Southeast Asia

Country	Rollback completed	Mode of labor control after rollback	Union/party landscape	Union density
Indonesia	Mid-1960s	Authoritarian state	Mono-union (SPSI) with weak links to ruling party	2.6[a]
Malaysia	Mid-1950s	Authoritarian state	Multi-union, MTUC dominant but not linked to ruling party	8.3[b]
Philippines	Mid-1950s	Employer (mid-1950s–1972, 1986–2000) Authoritarian state (1972–86)	Multi-union but TUCP favored by Marcos dictatorship	12.3[b]
Singapore	Mid-1960s	Authoritarian state	Mono-union (NTUC) linked to ruling PAP	15.7[b]
Thailand	Mid-1950s	Authoritarian state (1958–73) Despotic market (late 1970s–2000)	No unions under Sarit, multi-union thereafter	3.1[a]

[a] As percentage of the nonagricultural workforce in 1995.
[b] As percentage of the total workforce in 2000.

Source: The 1995 data are from the International Labour Organization (1997); the 2000 data are from the *Foreign Labor Trends* reports prepared by the US Department of Labor.

noncommunist western unions soon exited the WFTU to join the International Confederation of Free Trade Unions (ICFTU) in 1949. After this, the WFTU became more firmly aligned with the eastern bloc (Carew 1996; Devinatz 2013; Weiler 1981). The affinity of the strongest unions in the region for the WFTU confirmed western powers' worst fears. As the Cold War heated up in the late 1940s and early 1950s, the confrontation between the western and eastern blocs became intertwined with the efforts of conservative elites in Southeast Asia to defeat leftist groups that challenged them for control of new nation-states. The rollback of the left took longer to accomplish in some countries than in others, but governments in the region ultimately succeeded in eliminating leftists and their affiliated labor organizations as significant organized forces.

Among the countries that contained the left by the mid-1950s was the Philippines. During the war, the main resistance to the Japanese occupation was a peasant-based movement, the Hukbalahap (or the Huks), which fought along-side returning US forces in 1944 to expel the Japanese. After defeating Japan, the Americans disarmed the Huks and granted independence to the Philippines in 1946 (Kerkvliet 1977). With the transition to independent rule, the urban and rural organizations that were part of the united front against Japan retooled for competition in democratic elections and formed the Democratic Alliance (DA). Among the groups that coalesced into the DA were labor organizations, of which the Congress of Labor Organization (CLO) was the most powerful (Dejillas 1994; Ramos 1976; Wurfel 1959). The DA competed in the April 1946 congressional races and overcame vicious attacks from landed oligarchs and the military police to elect six candidates. The Speaker of the House prevented them from taking their seats, however, and soon the Huks were in open revolt (Kerkvliet 1977). With US support, the government waged a counterinsurgency war against the Huks and cracked down on other left-wing organizations, including the CLO.[1] After suspending the CLO's registration and imprisoning its leadership, the government sponsored new, more easily controlled unions (Ramos 1976; Wurfel 1959). By the end of the 1950s, a labor movement that had been largely class-based and politically oriented became "conservatively economistic and somewhat coopted into the system" (Ramos 1976, 33).

In the British colonies of Malaya and Singapore, leftists and their affiliated unions were especially strong at the end of the war. There, ethnic Malay elites had cooperated with the Japanese, and it was the Communist Party of Malaya (CPM) that led the fight against the Japanese and served as the de facto governing authority before Britain's reassertion of power in September 1945

---

[1] In addition to concerns about communist infiltration, the United States also sought to protect its substantial business interests and bases. The DA had pledged to limit US influence in the archipelago (Kerkvliet 1977).

(Stenson 1970; Trocki 2001). Among the groups that seized the postwar moment of political opportunity, perhaps the most assertive were the CPM-linked unions – the Pan-Malayan Federation of Trade Unions (PMFTU) and the Singapore Federation of Trade Unions (SFTU) – which mobilized thousands of workers in an "unparalleled wave of strikes" (Fong and Tan 1983; Morgan 1977, 170). These disruptions prompted a backlash from employers that further escalated the conflict and culminated with the CPM mounting an armed rebellion against the colonial state. The British declared a state of emergency in 1948 and the leadership of CPM-affiliated unions went underground (Jomo and Todd 1994; Stenson 1970). By the time Malaya became independent in 1957, the CPM was a rag-tag force hiding in the jungle and the British had supplanted the PMFTU with "responsible" unions affiliated to the Malayan Trade Union Congress (MTUC) (Fong and Tan 1983; Rudner 1973). The labor movement would never "be as strong as in the immediate postwar years, numerically or politically" (Morgan 1977, 185).

In neighboring Singapore, it was the People's Action Party (PAP) and not the British that quashed the left. Shunning the pro-government unions that the British established in the late 1950s, workers flocked to militant organizations (Trocki 2001). Although these unions initially aligned with the PAP, they switched allegiances after leftist PAP cadres resigned and formed a new social-ist party, the Barisan Sosialis, in the wake of the PAP's victory in the 1959 elections. The PAP's leader, Lee Kuan Yew, responded by attacking leftist opponents, deregistering assertive unions, and shepherding the remaining unions into the state-backed National Trade Union Centre (NTUC, later Congress) (Deyo 1989; Luther 1978). As in Malaya, with the government's having purged the militants from the labor movement, "strike action, confrontation and worker militancy were things of the past" (Trocki 2001, 128).

This general pattern of leftist groups seizing political opportunities during the early postwar period, followed by rollback, unfolded in Thailand as well. Unlike its neighbors, Thailand had not been colonized. With conquest by Japan inevitable, most of Thailand's political elites chose to cooperate with Japan. Among the Thais who resisted the Japanese occupation was Pridi Phanomyong, one of the architects of the 1932 overthrow of Siam's absolute monarchy. Pridi founded the Sahachip (Cooperative) Party, which competed in elections in Thailand's revived parliamentary institutions and dominated civilian govern-ments from 1944 to 1947. During this period, working-class groups began to organize as well, most prominently the left-leaning Association of United Workers of Thailand (AUWT).[2] The AUWT's leaders belonged to several

---

[2] This organization is also commonly referred to as the Central Labor Union (CLU).

parties, including the Communist Party, but they backed Pridi's party in elections. Pridi served briefly as prime minister in 1946, but he resigned after Thailand's young king died from a mysterious gunshot wound. As the political scene became more chaotic, the military intervened and overthrew the civilian government in 1947, then proceeded to crack down on the AUWT and other organizations allied with Pridi. Due to his anti-Japanese war record, the Americans had initially favored Pridi over conservative forces in Thailand, but after the Viet Minh took up arms against the French in neighboring Indochina, Thailand became a frontline country in the Cold War and the Americans changed allegiances, throwing their support behind a series of military regimes (Hewison 2020).[3] Initially, military governments permitted labor organizing and even sponsored trade unions, but after General Sarit took power in the twin coups of 1957 and 1958, he imprisoned key labor leaders and banned labor organizations, effectively shutting down most labor mobilization for years to come (Brown 2003; Glassman 2004).

Indonesia was the last to stamp out leftist organizations and their affiliated unions. One reason for this is that the Indonesian Communist Party (*Partai Komunis Indonesia*, PKI) was in a weakened state when the war against the Dutch ended. Noncommunist nationalist forces had crushed a rebellion by communist militias in 1948, which provided leading nationalists with strong anti-communist credentials. After independence, President Sukarno adopted a nonaligned posture on the global stage and permitted the PKI to regroup. They soon began to participate in the new nation's parliamentary system of governance (Kahin and Kahin 1995; Mortimer 2006). Among the plethora of labor unions active in the early postwar period, the PKI-aligned All-Indonesian Federation of Workers' Organizations (*Sentral Organisasi Buruh Seluruh Indonesia*, SOBSI) was the most powerful (Hawkins 1971; Tedjasukmana 1958). The PKI proved to be adept at electoral competition, winning 15 percent of the national parliamentary seats in 1955, and increasing its share of the vote in the 1957 local elections. The PKI became the largest nonruling communist party in the world and began to challenge both the military in nationalized Dutch enterprises and landowners in the countryside (Mortimer 2006). The Indonesian military and American officials became increasingly concerned that Indonesia would fall into communist hands (Kahin and Kahin 1995).[4] The US

---

[3] Pridi's royalist and military opponents accused him of being a communist, a charge that the United States came to accept, and which became more persuasive after he fled to China (Hewison 2020).

[4] These fears led the Americans to support a group of rebellious colonels based in the outer islands in the late 1950s. This endeavor failed spectacularly, further stoking anti-American sentiment (Kahin and Kahin 1995).

directed substantial resources to anti-PKI generals, and after a failed coup attempt in 1965, General Suharto rallied the PKI's opponents to slaughter the party and its affiliated groups (Roosa 2006; Simpson 2008).[5] By the time Suharto shunted Sukarno aside to become president in 1967, the military and its allies had obliterated the PKI and SOBSI.

2.1.2 Phase II: Containing Labor

Once militant unions vanished from the scene, capitalist regimes in the region ramped up their industrialization drives. Defanging unions had the added benefit, from the perspective of ruling elites, of aiding the rapid expansion of labor-intensive industries that fueled export-oriented industrialization (Hadiz 1997; Rodan et al. 2001). Wages comprised a significant share of production costs in these industries, and exports faced stiff competition in world markets. Cost containment was a paramount concern.[6] Before this economic transformation, union members worked primarily in plantations, docks, mines, transportation, the civil service, and the small number of large manufacturing companies (both private and state-owned) (Deyo 2001). As can be seen in Table 2, industry contributed less than 20 percent of GDP in 1960 in all countries except the Philippines, while agriculture accounted for a large share of GDP in all countries except Singapore. In terms of employment, agriculture absorbed well over half the labor force in all countries but Singapore (see Table 3). As industrialization

Table 2 Share of agriculture and industry in GDP

	Agriculture			Industry[a]		
	1960	**1980**	**1994**	**1960**	**1980**	**1994**
Indonesia	45	24	17	17	42	41
Malaysia	40	22	14	18	38	43
Philippines	26	25	22	28	39	33
Singapore	4	1	0	18	38	36
Thailand	40	23	10	19	29	39

[a] Includes mining, manufacturing, construction, and electricity, water, and gas industries
Source: World Bank (1978, 1996).

---

[5] This coup remains one of the most controversial episodes in Indonesian history, and scholars continue to disagree about the primary actors behind it. For excellent summaries, see Roosa (2006) and Robinson (2020).

[6] See Kuruvilla (1996) for an analysis of the connection between industrialization and industrial relations regimes.

Table 3 Share of labor force in agriculture and industry

	Agriculture			Industry[a]		
	1960	**1980**	**1994**	**1960**	**1980**	**1994**
Indonesia	68	58	46	8	12	19
Malaysia	56	41	21	12	19	32
Philippines	61	52	45	10	15	15
Singapore	9	2	0	21	42	33
Thailand	82	71	56	4	10	18

[a] Includes mining, manufacturing, construction, and electricity, water, and gas industries
Source: World Bank (1996, 1976) and World Development Indicators database.

progressed, agriculture's share of GDP and employment diminished, while industry's share of GDP and employment increased.

Economic transformations created the raw material for a resurgence of labor organizations, but "nowhere spawned effective trade unionism or enhanced worker participation in political or economic arenas" (Deyo 2001, 265). One reason for this outcome is that after rolling back the left, governments in capitalist Southeast Asia erected systems of labor control that prevented the revival of militant unions. Most countries adopted "authoritarian state" models of labor control that deployed legal and extra-legal techniques to prevent or curtail worker activism (Anner 2015). Indonesia, Singapore, Malaysia, and the Philippines under Marcos fall in this authoritarian state category. The specific features of their labor control regimes varied (e.g., some were corporatist, others were not), but in all cases, the state was the primary agent of labor control.[7] In countries that were more democratic, labor control regimes conformed more closely to "despotic market" and "employer" modes of labor control (Anner 2015). In these two modes of labor control, the state still plays an important role, but the locus of labor control shifts to the market or the employer. In despotic market regimes, the whip of the market – for example, the fear of job loss – is the primary means of curtailing labor militancy. In employer-based regimes, employers deploy preemptive measures such as forming yellow unions or buying-off union leaders, and retaliatory actions like firing organizers or hiring goons to beat them up. Thailand hews most closely to the despotic market model

---

[7] Frenkel makes a useful distinction between Singapore, which he designates as state corporatist because unions are controlled by the state but included in decision-making bodies, and "state exclusionary" systems in Thailand and Malaysia, where unions were not incorporated into decision-making bodies. The Philippines under Marcos and Indonesia under Suharto fit some-what awkwardly into this typology because they have elements of both – they were state corporatist in that the state fostered a union and included it on tripartite bodies, but they also utilized state exclusionary methods (Caraway 2004; Ford 1999; Hadiz 1997; Hutchison 2015).

and pre- and post-Marcos Philippines to the employer model. Despite these differences in labor control regimes, the result was the same: unions neither challenged the model of accumulation nor incubated the left. Across the board, unions were largely enterprise based, organized a small proportion of the workforce, and with a few notable exceptions, did not mobilize on a scale that threatened to disrupt the labor control regime.

Of the four cases of authoritarian state labor control, Malaysia is the only one that did not establish state-backed unions. After becoming independent in 1957, a coalition of ethnically based parties, Barisan Nasional, led by the United Malays National Organization (UMNO), governed the country. UMNO did not officially back the dominant labor center bequeathed to it from the British, the MTUC (which was renamed the Malaysian Trade Union Congress). Instead of erecting corporatist institutions to control the labor movement, the Malaysian state relied primarily on legal administrative techniques to rein in militant unions. During this period, Malaysia's unions were more autonomous than in the other cases of authoritarian state labor control and still evinced some occasional feistiness into the 1960s. When the number of strikes surged in the early 1960s, however, the government deregistered the striking unions and tightened registration requirements to prevent the formation of large unions that could mount disruptive actions (Todd and Jomo 1988).[8] The government also used its emergency powers to impose further restrictions on unions that prevented them from participating in politics (Todd and Jomo 1988, 117–19).[9] These steps kept unions in check. In subsequent years the government continued to utilize administrative measures, divide-and-rule tactics, and the selective targeting of troublesome leaders. For example, during the Malaysian Air Systems (MAS) dispute of 1978–9, the government arrested and detained union leaders under the Internal Security Act, deregistered the union, dismissed workers, and amended labor laws to raise further barriers to striking (Dunkley 1982; Jomo and Todd 1994, 146–48; Rowley and Bhopal 2006, 102–3). In the 1980s, the government punished the MTUC for flirting with an UMNO breakaway party by recognizing the civil servant union as a rival labor center and sponsoring an alternative trade-union center, the Malaysian Labor Organization (MLO) (Rowley and Bhopal 2006, 104; Todd and Jomo 1988).[10] Malaysia's system of ethnically based political

---

[8] In 1962 and 1964, there were ninety-five and eighty-five strikes, respectively, involving over 200,000 workers (Jomo and Todd 1994, 48).

[9] This new restriction was in response to the MTUC backing thirteen candidates from several political parties that had endorsed their "Workers Charter" in the 1969 elections. Nine of the candidates won their races (Jomo and Todd 1994).

[10] The MTUC's flirtation with the breakaway party was a response to the government's promotion of in-house unions as part of its "Look East" policy. After the MLO failed to dislodge the MTUC, however, UMNO's Anwar Ibrahim persuaded the Malay president of the MTUC to join UMNO.

parties also facilitated UMNO's containment project – the party's championing of Malay opportunity weakened the resonance of class-based appeals among Malays, and the MTUC risked stoking communal tensions if it aligned with non-Malay parties (Arudsothy and Littler 1993; Bhopal 2001).

Singapore's PAP utilized similar techniques to UMNO but combined them with corporatist methods of control and cooptation. After Singapore's exit from the Federation of Malaysia in 1965,[11] the PAP put a decisive end to its remaining opponents on the left, deregistering militant unions and arresting their leaders (Deyo 1989). To ensure labor's domestication, the PAP nurtured the NTUC as the only legally recognized peak labor center and cultivated a tight interconnection between the union and the party.[12] Union officials served as PAP MPs and held government portfolios; PAP MPs also served on the NTUC's Central Committee (Barr 2000; Leggett 1988, 247). This interlocking leadership between the party and the NTUC gave the union a voice in policymaking, but it also harnessed organized labor behind the regime's economic agenda. The NTUC, far from being a squeaky wheel, supported the government in its productivist agenda of stabilizing labor costs, increasing productivity, and maintaining labor peace (Deyo 2001). The government also made it virtually impossible to strike legally, and very few strikes occurred after 1965 (Leggett 1993).[13] To ensure labor's continued docility, the government initiated an in-house union policy in the early 1980s, over the objection of many NTUC leaders (Leggett 1988). Unions that stepped out of line faced the full wrath of the state. The starkest example was the suppression of the Singapore Airline Pilots' Association, which was not affiliated to the NTUC, for conducting an illegal work-to-rule action in 1980–1. Prime Minister Lee Kuan Yew infamously took charge of the labor dispute, subjecting the unions' leadership to public humiliation and threatening to shut down the airline permanently. The authorities charged several union leaders for organizing an illegal industrial action, and the union soon found its registration revoked. The NTUC, which had berated the pilots throughout the dispute, soon established a new pilots' union that excluded expatriate pilots, who were scapegoated by the government (Leggett 1984). Such scorched earth tactics sent a clear message. Through suppression, then administrative and corporatist controls, the regime tamed what was perhaps the

---

After this the MLO disbanded and its member unions joined the MTUC (Bhopal 2001, 91; Rowley and Bhopal 2006).

[11] Singapore became self-governing in 1959, and then formed the Federation of Malaysia with Malaya, North Borneo, and Sarawak in 1963.

[12] In 1963, 64 percent of organized workers belonged to the NTUC; by 1979, 95 percent were members (Leggett 1988).

[13] From 1966 to 1969 and from 1970 to 1979, twenty-eight and forty-four strikes occurred. In the next decade (1980–9), only two strikes took place (Leggett 1993, 121).

most contentious working class in the region and assured that it would challenge neither PAP rule nor the party's economic agenda.

In Indonesia, Suharto's New Order regime also sought to deter future working-class mobilization by establishing a system of corporatist controls (Ford 1999; Hadiz 1997). The organizational form of the new labor regime began to take shape in 1973 when authorities consolidated the surviving noncommunist unions into a state-controlled federation, the All-Indonesia Labor Federation (*Federasi Buruh Seluruh Indonesia*, FBSI, renamed the All-Indonesia Workers' Union [*Serikat Pekerja Seluruh Indonesia*, SPSI] in 1985). Although SPSI held a de facto monopoly on organizing in the private sector,[14] the regime took steps to assure that it did not become too strong. SPSI received minimal financial support, making union leaders easy targets for cooptation by employers and local officials (Hadiz 1997; Kammen 1997). Unlike in neighboring Singapore, however, the ruling Golkar party did not develop organic links with the state-backed union (Hadiz 1997). The state also placed tight legal restrictions on strikes, deployed the intelligence apparatus to thwart protests, dispersed strikes when they did occur, and used harsh measures against strike leaders (Hadiz 1997; Indonesian Documentation and Information Centre 1981; Tanter 1990). These steps were effective until the early 1990s when illegal independent unions began to gain traction and a wave of wildcat strikes erupted in industrial areas around Indonesia (Ford 2009; Kammen 1997). Increased scrutiny of labor rights abuses by the international community and the non-radical nature of worker demands led the regime to restore labor peace with a combination of carrots and sticks. To address workers' grievances, the government implemented higher minimum wages but cracked down on the leaders of independent unions (Glasius 1999; Kammen 1997; Manning 1998). These measures quelled labor unrest, and when anti-regime protests broke out in 1997–8, organized labor was not a driving force behind them (Aspinall 1999).

Containment took a different path in the Philippines and Thailand. In part because these countries experienced more years of democracy than their neighbors, authoritarian state methods of labor control were not the predominant mode. In the years before Marcos declared martial law in 1972, employers, not the state, were the primary agents of labor control. Labor legislation enacted in the early 1950s created a framework for business unionism centered on enterprise-based collective bargaining. Many workplace unions were yellow unions established and/or dominated by management, and since national unions were organizationally

---

[14] The law did not explicitly grant SPSI a representational monopoly, but registration requirements prevented independent unions from acquiring legal recognition.

fragmented, ideologically divided, nonpolitical, and often led by labor lawyers who viewed workers as clients, employer-led methods of labor control were sufficient to keep labor in check (Hutchison 2015; Ramos 1976; Snyder and Nowak 1982). Most union members were not covered by collective bargaining agreements and had never gone on strike (Snyder and Nowak 1982). After Marcos declared martial law, the state supplanted employers as the main agent of labor control. Marcos set up a semi-corporatist system with a state-backed labor center, the Trade Union Congress of the Philippines (TUCP), at its center. Marcos placed limitations on strikes, restricted collective bargaining with compulsory arbitration, and used tripartism and other perquisites to coopt labor leaders (Hutchison 2015; Torres-Yu 2003).

After Marcos's fall and the return to democracy, the state's role in labor control diminished once again, but the social forces unleashed by the mass movement to overthrow Marcos threatened oligarchic dominance and resulted in a harsher version of the pre-Marcos labor control regime. Significantly, during the late Marcos years, the left re-emerged as a force in Philippine politics. The Maoist Communist Party of the Philippines (CPP), and its armed wing, the New People's Army, developed into a full-blown insurgency (Boudreau 2004; Quimpo 2008). Small leftist organizations that had gone underground after the declaration of martial law also grew in strength and became part of the broad mass-based resistance to the regime in the early 1980s (Boudreau 2004). On the labor front as well, militant organizers coalesced into a progressive labor center, the Kilusang Mayo Uno (KMU), which organized a wave of strikes after martial law was lifted in 1981 (Dejillas 1994; Torres-Yu 2003). Labor was an important participant in the anti-Marcos People Power movement. Even the TUCP in the end abandoned Marcos. The incoming Aquino administration rewarded labor by appointing an ally of the radical unions as Minister of Labor. Aquino also revoked some of the regressive decrees from the Marcos years and raised minimum wages. This honeymoon period ended, however, after a failed military coup. As Aquino moved to secure her right flank, she sacked the progressive Minister of Labor and cracked down on strikes (Magadia 2003). In the end, the diverse coalition that brought Marcos down was no match for the oligarchs, who quickly regrouped and recaptured the majority of elected offices, effectively thwarting any hope of further pro-labor legislative reforms (Anderson 1988; Hutchison 2015). Labor control became increasingly decentralized and often violent, with local governments and racketeering unions colluding with employers to deter independent organizing (Sidel 1998). Consequently, despite the seemingly propitious conditions for the emergence of a strong labor movement in the 1980s, ruling classes quickly reestablished control. Organized labor under democratic rule was not stronger, and was perhaps weaker, than under Marcos (Hutchison 2015).

In Thailand, authoritarian controls on labor broke down in the 1970s and were replaced by less overt but arguably longer-lasting methods. After Sarit's death in 1963, generals Thanom Kittikachorn and Praphas Charusathien took power. As Thailand was sucked deeper into the vortex of the expanding war in Indochina, it became a "gigantic immobile aircraft carrier," hosting nearly 60,000 US troops and operating at least eight large bases (Anderson 1977, 15). The war propelled an economic boom that deeply transformed Thai society and created fertile recruiting conditions for the Communist Party of Thailand (CPT) among the impoverished peasantry; by the end of the 1960s, the CPT posed a serious threat to the regime (Morell and Chai'anan 1981). As the war in Indochina wound down, the economy nosedived and students took to the streets to bring down the military regime in October 1973. The three-year democratic interregnum that followed opened the floodgates to labor mobilization, and many new unions formed. Workers forged alliances with students, engaged in over a thousand strikes, and participated in numerous protests (Brown 2003; Mabry and Srisermbhok 1985; Wehmhorner 1983). To provide a legal frame-work for industrial relations, the government enacted a new law, the 1975 Labor Relations Act (LRA), which accorded workers the right to strike, to bargain collectively, and to establish unions. The explosion of contentiousness, how-ever, soon prompted a conservative backlash, and in October 1976 a military coup brought an end to this period of more assertive labor activism. Leaders of radical labor organizations faced arrest, imprisonment, and harassment. Many fled to the jungles to join the CPT (Brown 2003).

In the aftermath of the coup, the military government suppressed militant organizations but soon eased restrictions on labor, offered amnesty to CPT members, and refrained from taking harsh measures against striking workers (Mabry and Srisermbhok 1985; Wehmhorner 1983, 484). The number of regis-tered unions increased, but labor remained relatively weak because no strong labor centers existed (Ativanichayapong 2002). The LRA, which the military did not revoke, facilitated this outcome by forcing unions to stay focused on workplace concerns and fostering a proliferation of competing organizations (Brown 2003). Over time, the labor movement became extremely fragmented, with the largest federations locked in internecine conflict (Brown 2003; Mabry and Srisermbhok 1985, 627; Piriyarangsan and Poonpanich 1994).[15] The mili-tary also actively sought to sow divisions among unions by establishing its own organizations and promoting fractional disputes in the stronger labor centers (Brown 2003, 102–4; Mabry and Srisermbhok 1985). The military relinquished its direct hold on power in 1988, but when it briefly reclaimed power in 1991–2,

---

[15] There were nine national labor congresses and eleven sectoral federations (Robertson 2001, 98).

it further weakened unions by banning state enterprise worker unions, which were the strongest element within organized labor (Brown 2003).[16] With no tangible threat from the left, a fragmented labor movement, and large reserves of rural labor, a despotic market mode of labor control was sufficient to keep Thailand's weak and fragmented unions in check.

Through these varied techniques of control – state authoritarian, employer, and despotic market – authoritarian and democratic regimes in capitalist Southeast Asia successfully contained labor. Although labor militancy occasionally broke out, states intervened with both co-optative and suppressive measures to restore "labor peace." As a result, at the dawn of the twenty-first century, unions in these countries were too weak and fragmented, or too co-opted, to pose a challenge to these regimes and their mode of accumulation. In non-capitalist Southeast Asia, the outcome was similar, but the pathway followed to get there was distinct.

2.2 War, Socialism, and Economic Liberalization: Cambodia, Laos, Myanmar, and Vietnam

Years of war and economic isolation resulted in a distinct postwar trajectory in socialist Southeast Asia. In Indochina – Cambodia, Laos, and Vietnam – the wars with France and then the United States embroiled these countries in conflict for more than two decades. When the war finally ended in 1975, communist parties seized power. In Laos and Vietnam, communist parties embarked on conventional programs of socialist economic development, but in Cambodia, the victorious Khmer Rouge emptied the cities and unleashed a genocide that killed almost 2 million people (Beresford 2006; Kiernan 2002; Stuart-Fox 1986). Myanmar, by contrast, was comparatively free from Cold War bloodletting, but after the military seized power in 1962, it isolated the country from the rest of the world and pursued an idiosyncratic "Burmese path to socialism." The government nationalized large private businesses and the state assumed control over all distribution, exporting, and importing of goods (Silverstein 1977). Yet as can be seen in Table 4, despite these being "workers' states," there were startling parallels with labor in capitalist Southeast Asia. Unions organized a small proportion of the workforce and authoritarian state labor controls predominated.

Low union density in these countries was primarily an effect of the overwhelming dominance of agriculture in socialist economies. War in Indochina and closure to the outside world in Myanmar also had profound consequences for the size of the

---

[16] Thailand partially restored these rights in 2000, well after the return to democracy, largely as a result of the US's threat to revoke trade privileges (Robertson 2001).

Table 4 Labor control in socialist Southeast Asia

Country	Mode of labor control	Union/party landscape	Union density (2000) (as % of the total workforce)
Cambodia	Authoritarian state/ Despotic market	Multi-union with some unions linked to ruling party	1.0
Laos	Authoritarian state	Mono-union (LFTU) linked to ruling party	–
Myanmar	Authoritarian state	Mono-union linked to ruling party (1962–88)/ No unions (1988–2000)	0
Vietnam	Authoritarian state	Mono-union (VGCL) linked to ruling party	10.0

Source: *Foreign Labor Trends* reports, US Department of Labor, for union density. Data unavailable for Laos.

industrial working class. Agriculture still contributed a significant proportion of GDP and employed well over 60 percent of the workforce in all four countries in the 1990s (see Tables 5 and 6). The potential for working-class mobilization was therefore more limited than in capitalist Southeast Asia.

Like authoritarian governments in capitalist nations, socialist parties also deployed authoritarian state methods of labor control, but with important differences. In Laos and Vietnam, communist parties recognized unions and integrated them into the party state with near-universal membership in state-run industries. In Myanmar and Cambodia, there was more variation over time. Myanmar's military regime initially organized worker associations but then banned all unions, while in Cambodia, despotic market modes of labor control prevailed by the end of the twentieth century as a consequence of international intervention in the 1990s.

In unified Vietnam, the Vietnamese Communist Party (VCP) initially ran the economy on socialist principles. As is typical in countries governed by communist parties, the party-backed union functioned as a "transmission belt" between the party and workers. Although formally independent from the VCP, the Vietnam General Confederation of Labor (VGCL) was subordinate to the party and tightly integrated into its structures (Hansson 2003; Schweisshelm and Chi 2018). In the workplace, the VGCL participated in enterprise management, channeled benefits to workers, and mobilized them to

Table 5 Share of agriculture and industry in GDP

	Agriculture			Industry[a]		
	1960	**1980**	**1994**	**1960**	**1980**	**1994**
Cambodia	51	–	51[b]	17	–	14[b]
Lao PDR	–	–	51	–	–	18
Vietnam	–	–	28	–	–	30
Myanmar	33	47	63	12	13	9

[a] Includes mining, manufacturing, construction, and electricity, water, and gas industries
[b] 1995, value added as share of GDP
Source: World Bank (1978, 1996, 1997).

Table 6 Share of labor force in agriculture and industry

	Agriculture			Industry[a]		
	1960	**1980**	**1994**	**1960**	**1980**	**1994**
Cambodia	–	–	79	–	–	6
Lao PDR	–	80	86	–	6	3
Vietnam	–	73	68	–	13	11
Myanmar	63	76	69	11	8	10

[a] Includes mining, manufacturing, construction, and electricity, water, and gas industries
Source: World Bank (1996, 1976) and World Development Indicators Database.

meet production targets. Workplace conflicts were dealt with through negotiations at the enterprise level (Beresford and Nyland 1998; Hansson 2003; Nørlund 2004). Economic reforms in the 1980s provided more scope for private enterprise, including foreign investment. As the private sector expanded, Vietnamese workers increasingly labored in private firms, and state-owned enterprises began to be run along capitalist principles. VGCL cadres were ill-prepared to deal with the inevitable disputes that arose between workers and management in the private sector. Many workplaces in the private sector were not unionized, and even when they were, plant-level union leaders often continued to serve as managers or as party cell leaders (Edwards and Phan 2008; Hansson 2003). With the VGCL absent or co-opted, workers began to organize wildcat actions to seek redress for their mounting grievances. Only after conflicts emerged did the VCP dispatch VGCL cadres to mediate, and these interventions typically resulted in some worker demands being met (Beresford and Nyland 1998; Hansson 2003; Schweisshelm and Chi 2018). In Vietnam's system of authoritarian state labor control, then, the VGCL was tightly wed to the ruling party and therefore had a more prominent political role than unions in most of capitalist Southeast Asia. But it had shallow roots in the working class, leaving the VGCL to function as a firefighter when labor disputes occurred in the growing private sector.

In Laos as well, the Lao People's Revolutionary Party adopted a transmission belt model of authoritarian state labor control. As in Vietnam, the party recognized one peak organization, the Lao Federation of Trade Unions (LFTU), which was both subordinate to and organically linked to the party. Laos also adopted economic reforms in the 1980s, but it was unsuccessful in attracting significant foreign investment, and most union members continued to be in the state sector. Strikes were rare, which was likely due to the fact that so few people worked in industry (Fry 2008).

In contrast to Laos and Vietnam, where stable communist regimes came into being after the end of the Vietnam War, the Khmer Rouge's reign in Cambodia brought more than a decade of economic and political instability. Vietnam invaded Cambodia in 1978 and ousted the Khmer Rouge from power, but the ensuing geopolitical infighting between China, Vietnam, and the United States, and the continuing war to stamp out the remaining Khmer Rouge forces, put a brake on economic development. When Vietnamese forces left in 1989, they handed power to their Cambodian allies, Hun Sen's Cambodian People's Party (CPP), which worked with a UN transitional authority in 1992–3 to establish a pluralist constitutional regime. Elections in 1993 brought a coalition government to power, but Hun Sen staged a coup in 1997, and the CPP has been in power ever since (Hall 2000). Cambodia also liberalized its economy and attracted significant East Asian investment in the garment industry (Arnold and Shih 2010; Hall 2000; Polaski 2006). At the time, there were no worker organizations of significance in the private sector and opposition parties cultivated these workers as a potential base of support (Nuon and Serrano 2010). When the first wave of worker protests began in 1996, the opposition Sam Rainsy Party supported the formation of the Free Trade Union of Workers of the Kingdom of Cambodia and advocated for pro-labor policies such as raising the minimum wage (Hughes 2007). In response, the Hun Sen regime sponsored pro-regime unions, refused to register independent unions, intimidated protesting workers, and stood by as employers retaliated against labor activists (Hall 2000). But a trade agreement reached with the United States in 1999 conditioned textile export quotas on respect for labor rights, and as a result the regime granted legal status to several independent unions (Hall 2000; Polaski 2006).[17]

---

[17] In 1998, thirty-two different garment unions were registered with the Ministry of Labor; only three were free of government or management domination. The primary regime-backed union

Thus, at the end of the twentieth century, Cambodia was the only country among the (previously) socialist nations to have independent worker associations, and this fragile foothold was largely due to the unique conditions surrounding the development of the garment industry. With employers' and the state's hands tied to some extent by the international monitoring of labor conditions, market despotism became the dominant mode of labor control there.

Myanmar's postwar pathway was comparatively free of external intervention, but it was still tumultuous. After World War II, Myanmar was a parliamentary democracy and had a wide array of worker organizations, many of which were affiliated to political parties (Kyaw 2013). Parliamentary rule ended in 1962 after the military carried out a coup, and Ne Win's military regime sought to mobilize society behind his eccentric socialist vision. In support of this objective, the regime disbanded existing political parties and organizations and in their place created the Burma Socialist Program Party (BSPP) and a set of party-linked mass organizations, among them the People's Workers' Council (later known as the Workers' Association) (Silverstein 1977). The regime further tightened its control of labor after a strike wave in 1974, and labor contention diminished until the massive anti-regime protests of 1988 (Kyaw 2013).[18] Workers participated in the mass movement against the military, forming a new independent organization, the All Burma Labor Union, which organized general strikes and demanded the right to form independent worker associations (Arnold and Campbell 2017; Henry 2015). The regime organized elections in 1990, which it lost to the opposition that had rallied behind Aung San Suu Kyi's National League for Democracy (NLD), but it refused to cede power to civilians. The regime dismantled the Workers' Association, and labor activists that had formed alternative organizations went into exile.[19] In an attempt to revive the economy, the government issued a new foreign investment law and relaxed restrictions on private enterprise, but these measures failed to attract much manufacturing investment because of an international boycott of Burmese products (Kyaw 2013). At century's end, then, there were no legal unions in the country, and the economy remained overwhelmingly dependent on agriculture.

---

was the Independent Trade Union of Cambodian Workers, a descendant of the labor organization under Vietnamese rule (Hall 2000).

[18] The protests prompted Ne Win to resign, but the military did not relinquish power and rebranded itself as the State Law and Order Restoration Council (and later as the State Peace and Development Council).

[19] In exile they reassembled and formed the Free Trade Union of Burma (FTUB). From abroad, they worked with the international trade union movement to put a spotlight on labor rights abuses in Myanmar (Henry 2015).

2.3 Conclusion

As the twentieth century drew to a close, labor movements in Southeast Asia were not significant players in any country in the region. In capitalist Southeast Asia, governments rolled back the left and established systems of labor control that were highly effective in preventing the reemergence of working-class organizations that might challenge elites and the model of accumulation. In socialist Southeast Asia, economies were overwhelmingly dominated by agriculture after years of war and/or economic isolation, and most unions were subordinate to ruling parties. However, in the final years of the twentieth century, the economies of Cambodia and Vietnam were undergoing rapid change. With industrialization in labor-intensive export industries setting the stage for greater working-class mobilization there, and authoritarian state controls on labor relaxed in Indonesia and Timor-Leste after the fall of Suharto in May 1998, more favorable conditions for labor mobilization were developing in some countries. Section 3 assesses how these new developments affected systems of labor control established in the late twentieth century.

3 Continuity and Change in the Twenty-First Century

The story of organized labor in Southeast Asia during the late twentieth century was largely one of convergence: organized labor was weak and systems of labor control contained working-class mobilization throughout the region. This continues to be the case in much of the region in the twenty-first century. Unions still organize a small proportion of the workforce, are highly fragmented in many countries, and often fail to negotiate collective agreements. Aside from the few countries where ruling parties sponsored a single-party-linked organization, unions do not have strong ties to major political parties. But there are also important discontinuities. While workers in some countries remained relatively subdued (Laos, Malaysia, the Philippines, Singapore, and Thailand), strikes and labor protests became a more prominent feature in others (Cambodia, Indonesia, Myanmar, Timor-Leste, and Vietnam). Intriguingly, these patterns of contention cannot be explained by regime type, as workers remained relatively quiescent in some democracies, while workers in some autocracies and hybrid regimes frequently went on strike and organized protests.

I first analyze continuities in the region, focusing on persistent weaknesses in conventional measures of union power and grappling with the question of why organized labor in countries where unions are subordinate to ruling parties perform more strongly than the region's democracies on most indicators of union power. The stronger performance on these measures, I argue, is an artifact of the form of labor incorporation and not a reflection of labor's underlying power. I then analyze the forces driving higher labor contention in a subset of countries, arguing that economic and political transformations disrupted or ruptured old methods of labor control, creating fertile conditions for labor protest to re-emerge.

3.1 Continuities: Organizational Weakness

A striking pattern evident in Table 7 is that organized labor in Southeast Asia performs poorly on widely used measures of union power. Unionization rates are low, averaging about 9 percent. Even the highest unionization rate – Singapore at 21.2 percent – is hardly stellar. Throughout the region, bargaining takes place overwhelmingly at the enterprise level and the proportion of workers covered by collective bargaining agreements is lower than the unionization rate (Caraway 2010; Ford 2016; Fry and Mees 2016, 464; Leggett 2008, 112; Nuon and Serrano 2010, 35–36; Ofreneo 2020; Pringle and Clarke 2010; Wad 2019, 171; Ward and Mouyly 2016). When collective agreements are reached, they are often poor in quality and merely repeat existing labor law, do not cover wages, and even contain provisions that violate the law (Aganon et al. 2008, 2; Caraway 2010; Nuon and Serrano 2010, 35–36; Pringle and Clarke 2010, 97). Given the weakness of collective bargaining institutions, unions have increasingly relied on minimum wages rather than collective bargaining to increase member pay.[20] In about half of the countries in the region, organized labor is fragmented into many competing organizations and unaligned with a major political party.

The continued weakness of labor on these measures is not surprising in relatively autocratic settings where ruling parties held onto power and perpetuated existing systems of labor control. It is more surprising in democracies, which should provide a more amenable setting for unions to form, negotiate with employers, and engage openly in electoral politics and policy advocacy to advance workers' interests. Perplexingly, autocracies and hybrid regimes, on average, perform better than democracies on most of these measures of union power. I link these patterns to historical legacies from the containment phase and the timing of political transitions in countries that democratized.

Let us begin with the subset of countries where unions continue to be aligned with the ruling party – Laos, Vietnam, Singapore, and to a lesser extent, Cambodia. Party-sponsored unions in Laos, Singapore, and Vietnam continue to be tightly integrated into party structures in the twenty-first century. Top union leaders are party members, sit on important party committees, and hold cabinet positions

---

[20] All countries in the region except Singapore and Brunei have statutory minimum wages. In the rest of Southeast Asia, statutory minimum wages have existed since at least since 2000, with the exceptions of Malaysia, which introduced a minimum wage in 2013, and Myanmar, which revived its minimum wage after a long hiatus in 2013.

Table 7 Organized labor in Southeast Asia in the twenty-first century

	Unionization rate (% of employees)	Organizational concentration[a]	Collective bargaining coverage/ quality	Linked with ruling/major party?
Democracies				
Indonesia	7.0 (2012)	Low	Low	
Philippines	8.7 (2014)	Low	Low	
Timor-Leste	9 (2014)	Medium	Low	
Thailand[b]	3.5 (2015)	Low	Low	
Hybrid				
Cambodia (until 2017)	9.6 (2012)	Low	Low	X
Malaysia	8.8 (2016)	Medium	Low	
Myanmar (from 2011)	1 (2015)	Medium	Low	

Table 7 (cont.)

	Unionization rate (% of employees)	Organizational concentration[a]	Collective bargaining coverage/ quality	Linked with ruling/major party?
Singapore	21.2 (2015)	High	Low	X
Autocracies				
Laos	15.5 (2010)	High	Low	X
Vietnam	14.5 (2011)	High	Low	X

[a] Low = >5 peak labor centers/confederations; Medium = 2–5 peak labor centers/confederations; High = 1 peak labor center and few unaffiliated unions.

[b] Thailand is placed with democracies because this is the regime category it was in for the longest period.

Source: Beng and Tuan (2020), Do (2017), Ford (2016), Caraway and Ford (2020), Fry (2012), Gillan and Thein (2016), ILO Industrial Relations Database, Nuon and Serrano (2010), Ofreneo (2013), Thunyalak (2020), Wad (2020).

(Beng and Tuan 2020; Collins 2020; Fry 2008). Only one national peak association exists, to which all (or almost all in the case of Singapore) unions affiliate. This tight link between the party and the union has fostered both the highest unionization rates in Southeast Asia and high levels of organizational concentration.[21]

However, it would be a mistake to conclude that these unions are more powerful than those in neighboring countries. The comparatively high unionization and concentration rates reflect the ruling party's model of labor incorporation rather than organized labor's underlying power. The link between the official union and the ruling party gives union leaders a seat at the table in policy discussions, but their subordination to the party limits their ability to advocate for members. When the party's priorities collide with members' interests, union leaders become trapped in a "loyalty dilemma" (Burgess 2004). Loyalty to the party makes it difficult for union cadres to side with workers because ruling parties have the power to sanction disobedient union leaders. Since these are single-party-dominant regimes, union leaders do not have viable exit options. The mono-union setting also has consequences for union members. Since the party-backed union is the only union in town, they cannot show their dissatisfaction by joining a different union.

Little surprise, then, that the NTUC, LFTU, and VGCL do not break ranks with the party or cause trouble by organizing strikes. When strikes occur, they are wildcat actions taken without union support. In Singapore, the NTUC's leaders conduct their work in line with the PAP's view that trade unions should promote harmony and productivity in the workplace. The only ripples of industrial conflict during the last two decades were wildcat work stoppages by migrant workers in 2012 over poor living conditions and pay. Instead of defending the workers, the NTUC described one action as an "illegal strike" (Han 2018; Rajah 2019). Unlike Singapore, workers in Vietnam frequently strike. Although the VGCL evinces a more sympathetic posture to striking workers than the NTUC, it also avoids organizing industrial action. Laos's LFTU and Vietnam's VGCL have also on occasion politely advocated for higher minimum wages, and the VGCL opposed the government's proposed revisions to the Labor Code in 2012 and the Social Security Law in 2015, resulting in modifications to the government's proposal. Party backing, however, has not translated into quality collective agreements for union members.

---

[21] These countries also place fewer restrictions on unionization in state-linked employment, which contributes to their higher unionization rates. Exclusions of public sector workers from the right to unionize or bargain collectively affect large categories of workers in some countries. For example, civil servants do not have the right to unionize in Cambodia, Indonesia, and Thailand. Teachers in Cambodia and Thailand are also prohibited from unionizing.

In Cambodia, the ruling CPP also has links to unions, but in contrast to Laos, Singapore, and Vietnam, it has not imposed mono-unionism. As discussed in the previous section, the government agreed to permit independent unions to register alongside CPP-sponsored unions to gain access to western markets for its garment exports (Nuon and Serrano 2010).[22] Unionization rates and organizational concentration are therefore lower than in the countries where ruling parties sponsor a single union. Many unionized workplaces are also not covered by collective bargaining agreements, in part because multiple unions compete for members in a single workplace, which makes it more difficult to negotiate them.

In the rest of the region, ruling or major parties do not have strong links to unions, resulting in lower union density and a fragmented union landscape. Malaysia's ruling Barisan Nasional (BN) coalition, did not establish tight links to trade unions during the containment period, and this remains so today. Key features of Malaysia's restrictive labor laws have remained in place and continue to give the state legal tools to control and weaken unions. Unionization rates have declined further in the twenty-first century (Wad 2019).[23] It wasn't until Pakatan Harapan (PH) defeated the BN in the 2018 general elections that serious discussions began about transforming Malaysia's repressive controls on labor. The PH government made modest changes to the Industrial Relations Act, but reforms stalled after the government fell.[24] Even the PH government, however, availed itself of repressive provisions in the Societies Act to temporarily suspend the registration of Malaysia's largest labor organization, the MTUC, for alleged financial irregularities (Tee 2019).

In autocratic and hybrid regimes where ruling parties remained in power for most of the two decades thus far of the twenty-first century, the perpetuation of labor control regimes that they established, and the persistence of low unionization rates into the late twentieth century, is hardly surprising. Of the remaining five countries in the region, four have been democratic for much of or all the twenty-first century – Indonesia, the Philippines, Thailand, and Timor-Leste. Democratization often results in stronger collective labor rights

---

[22] In addition to legalizing independent unions, the regime also agreed to establish an independent Arbitration Council as an alternative to the corrupt courts and to permit the ILO to monitor labor standards.

[23] The government amended the Industrial Relations Act in 2007 and 2008, but these amendments did not fundamentally alter the labor control regime. The most significant amendment dropped the provision in the Industrial Relations Act that prohibited unions from negotiating conditions more favorable than those outlined in the Employment Act.

[24] For an analysis of amendments to the IRA, see the ILO's 2022 assessment: www.ilo.org/dyn/normlex/en/f?p=1000:13100:0::NO:13100:P13100_COMMENT_ID,P13100_COUNTRY_ID:412 2696,102960.

and more opportunities to advocate for pro-worker policies, which should, in theory, help labor to increase its ranks (Burgess 2010; Cook 2007; Caraway 2009; Cook 2007; Cook 2010). Organized labor's continued weakness on indicators of union power in the region's democracies therefore requires some explanation.

The timing of democratization partly explains why organized labor remains feeble. Democratic governments in the countries that democratized in the 1980s – the Philippines and Thailand – have far weaker protections for collective labor rights than countries that democratized later. The timing of democratization in the late 1980s – before the fall of the Soviet Union and the end of the Cold War – produced less propitious conditions for stronger pro-labor reforms. Memories of an armed left and popular social movements, moreover, were still fresh, and in the Philippines, the armed left was still an active presence. The Cold War era's containment logics were still in play, and new democratic governments refrained from rolling back many elements of labor law that constrained unions (Brown 2003; Magadia 2003).

However, after the Cold War ended, democratically elected governments in both the Philippines and Thailand still did not undertake significant labor reforms. Once the moment of democratic opening passed, opportunities for reform diminished. Existing regimes of labor control served ruling oligarchs well, and labor was too weak and divided to exert the pressure needed to make fundamental change.[25] Despite these similarities, there were also important differences in their labor control regimes. In the Philippines' untamed oligarchy, the intertwining of private and public violence, and impunity for perpetrators, created an especially toxic environment for labor that arguably worsened in the twenty-first century (Quimpo 2014). More than thirty years after the People Power revolution, workers who protest or go on strike often face arrest, trumped up criminal charges, intimidation, and beatings by hired thugs and the police (Global Labor Justice-International Labor Rights Forum 2021; Siwa and Viliran 2016). Since 2001, well over 100 labor activists have been killed extrajudicially (INDUSTRIALL 2020; Reuters 2009; Siwa

---

[25] Both countries qualify as "ruling oligarchies," that is, those who "command and control massive concentrations of material resources" also govern directly (Winters 2011, 6). Scholars have frequently applied an oligarchic lens to analyze politics in the Philippines – for a classic example, see Anderson (1988), and for more recent applications, see Winters (2011) and Quimpo (2014). Although Thai scholars seldom invoke the term (for an exception, see Rhoden (2015)), some of the most astute analyses of contemporary Thai politics have implicitly understood that the conflict between Thaksin Shinawatra and "network monarchy" is a battle between rival oligarchs (Kasian 2006; McCargo 2005). Despite being dubbed a "populist," Thaksin was filthy rich and pro-business. During his first term, he alienated much of organized labor when he rejected significant increases in the minimum wage and reneged on promises not to privatize state enterprises (Brown and Hewison 2004).

and Viliran 2016, 60). In one horrific case in November 2004, the army forcibly put down a strike at the Hacienda Luisita sugar mill and plantation owned by the family of former presidents Cory (1986–92) and Benigno Aquino III (2010–16), killing seven protestors (Orejas 2016). Little surprise, then, that union density, collective bargaining coverage, and strikes have plummeted from baselines that were already low (Amante 2019; Siwa and Viliran 2016).

In Thailand, the whip of the market rather than outright brutality is the main disciplining agent. For the more powerful state enterprise unions, however, stronger state controls are still in place. Democratic governments never fully restored their rights to bargain collectively or to strike. The most infamous recent example that illustrates the impact of these controls is the persecution of members of the State Railway Workers' Union of Thailand, which organized a health and safety campaign in the aftermath of a fatal railway accident in 2009. Members refused to operate trains without functioning safety features, and the courts ruled that the campaign was an illegal strike. The case dragged on for over a decade, resulting in hundreds of thousands of dollars in fines and three-year jail sentences for several union leaders and activists (Ratcliffe 2021). Since 2006, democratic governments have approved large increases in the minimum wage to win worker votes but have not made reforms that would create a better organizing environment for unions. Thailand's tumultuous politics since 2006 have also deepened divisions within the labor movement, with some siding with royalist yellow shirts and others with pro-Thaksin red shirts (Brown and Sakdina 2013; Ruji and Kriangsak 2021).

The other two democracies in the region underwent transitions in the late 1990s and early 2000s. By then, global attention to labor rights had exploded, and democratizing countries often invited the ILO to participate in drafting new labor legislation. Eager to dim the bright international spotlight on labor rights abuses, the Habibie administration in Indonesia invited the ILO to assist the government with revamping Indonesia's labor laws to bring them into closer alignment with international labor standards (Caraway 2004). In Timor-Leste, the United Nations transitional authority governed the country for several years after the 1999 referendum in which citizens voted to separate from Indonesia. During this time, the transitional authority issued a new Labor Code, drafted by the International Labour Organisation (Ford 2016). The ILO's involvement in recrafting labor laws resulted in much stronger protections for collective labor rights in these democracies than in the Philippines or Thailand (see Table 8).[26]

---

[26] Cambodia and Myanmar also invited the ILO to help draft its labor laws, resulting in stronger de jure protections than in the Philippines and Thailand as well as other hybrid regimes in the region (Bronstein 2005; Caraway 2009; Henry 2015). Although countries where the ILO participated in

Table 8 De jure legal restrictions on collective labor rights in 2020

	De jure collective rights (0–100)[a]	Union formation[b]	Collective bargaining[c]	Strikes[d]
Democracies				
Indonesia	83.6	Low	Low	High
Philippines	65	Medium	High	High
Timor-Leste	90	Low	Low	Medium
Thailand	60	High	Low	High
Hybrid				
Cambodia	81.4	Low	Low	High
Malaysia	58.6	High	High	High
Myanmar (2011–21)	77.1	Medium	Low	Medium
Singapore	65	High	High	High
Autocracies				
Laos	74.3	Medium	Medium	High
Vietnam	69.3	Medium	Low	High

[a] Higher scores indicate stronger protections for collective labor rights. See the Appendix for further information about the De Jure Collective Rights Index.

[b] Low = score <3; medium = scores 3–5; high = scores >5

[c] Low = scores 0–1; medium = scores 2; high = scores 3 or higher

[d] Low = scores 0–1; medium = scores 2; high = scores 3 or higher

Among the autocracies in the region, the most far-reaching political transformation occurred in Myanmar. The military government initiated a process of political opening in 2011 that had important consequences for trade unions. As part of the liberalization process, the government not only began to hold competitive elections – and permitted a civilian-led government to take office in 2015 – but also undertook other reforms designed to end Myanmar's political and economic isolation.[27] Myanmar had long been under fire for its appalling

---

the labor reform process have stronger protections for collective rights than other Southeast Asian nations, the ILO's liberal understanding of freedom of association also produced laws that facilitated organizational fragmentation, which can negatively affect the collective power of unions nationally – by dividing the labor movement – and at the plant level by pitting unions against each other (Caraway 2006).

[27] Myanmar was not fully democratic from 2011 to 2021 because the military retained control over internal and external security, was not subject to civilian oversight, and held reserved seats in parliament that allowed it to prevent changes to the constitution (Bünte 2022).

labor rights record; making improvements in this area would be an important precondition to the lifting of international sanctions. The Thein Sein government (2011–15) requested the ILO's assistance as it drafted new labor laws. In 2011, the legislature approved the Labor Organization Law legalizing trade unions (Henry 2015). Formerly exiled and underground labor activists soon began to organize unions (Gillan and Thein 2016; Henry 2015). Given that unions started from zero in 2011, and that much of population still works in agriculture, unions still organize a small proportion of the workforce despite the more conducive context for organizing.

The timing of democratization, however, had another consequence that pushed in the opposite direction of labor reforms in countries that transitioned later. The spread of precarious work in the wake of the Asian financial crisis hit these countries just as authoritarian restrictions on organizing lifted. Employers have increasingly turned to fixed-duration contracts, daily contracts, outsourcing, and subcontracting to avoid paying severance and providing other benefits to their workforce (Caraway 2009; Deyo 2012; Hewison and Tularak 2013; Juliawan 2010; Landau, Mahy, and Mitchell 2015; Ofreneo 2013; Serrano 2014; Tjandraningsih and Nugroho 2008). Although laws often limited the use of these arrangements, the authorities poorly enforce them (Caraway 2009; Human Rights Watch 2015; Lowenstein 2011; Serrano 2014). Precarity perpetuates the low preexisting levels of unionization by creating more difficult organizing conditions (Serrano 2014). Employers can simply not renew workers on short-term contracts who join unions, and workers employed by dispatch services cannot join unions in their workplaces because they do not have an employment contract with the end user of their labor.[28] These conditions affected all countries in the region – not just Indonesia, Malaysia, and Timor-Leste – and reinforced other economic and political factors that limited unions.

Although on average countries that democratized or liberalized later had stronger overall protections for collective rights than other countries in the region, there is one area where even countries that solicited assistance from the ILO did not make deep reforms: the right to strike. Here, the legacy of the past and the desire to limit disruptions to production conspired to stymie bolder reforms. As can be seen in Table 8, almost every country has high restrictions on the right to strike. Whereas democracies and countries that liberalized or democratized more recently fared better on de jure protections for establishing unions and collective bargaining, they did not provide stronger protections for

---

[28] Because of this, unions' members are usually permanent workers. For example, Tjandraningsih's (2013) study of the metal industry in Indonesia found that the overwhelming majority of union members were on permanent contracts. None of the outsourced workers belonged to a union, and only a few on short-term contracts had joined.

the right to strike. Myanmar and Timor-Leste, which reformed their labor laws most recently and where industrial relations institutions have the shortest history, have the fewest restrictions on the right to strike. Among the most common restrictions on strikes are lengthy conciliation and mediation processes (Cambodia, Indonesia, Laos, and Vietnam), strike votes that require the majority of a union's membership to approve strikes (Philippines, Myanmar, Singapore, Thailand; in Malaysia, two-thirds of members must approve a strike),[29] binding arbitration without the agreement of both parties (Indonesia, Laos, Malaysia, the Philippines, Singapore, Thailand, and Vietnam), and narrow definitions of disputes as workplace conflicts between workers and employers (Indonesia, Laos, Malaysia, Myanmar, the Philippines, Singapore, Thailand, Timor-Leste, Vietnam).[30]

As a consequence of these high barriers, most strikes in the region are illegal. Workers participating in illegal strikes face dismissal and in some cases, criminal sanctions that can result in imprisonment or heavy fines. Given this, it is unsurprising that workers in many Southeast Asian countries seldom strike. However, workers in some countries disregard these legal limitations and frequently strike. The next section analyzes the economic and political transformations that contributed to the emergence of more contentious labor movements in this subset of countries.

3.2 Change Amid Continuity: Rising Contentiousness

Why did workers in some countries in Southeast Asia become more contentious in the twenty-first century? Increased worker mobilization in countries that became more democratic is perhaps to be expected, but some of the most dramatic surges in strikes occurred in autocracies. I link rising contention to the effects of economic and political transformations on preexisting labor control regimes. In countries that experienced neither economic nor political change, old methods of containment held, and labor conflict remained subdued (see Figure 1). But where economic *or* political transformations occurred, existing labor control regimes either came under enormous stress or collapsed, which opened the door to more labor contention.

As outlined in the previous subsection, countries that underwent more recent regime transitions made deeper labor reforms than countries that democratized

---

[29] The ILO considers a membership majority vote to be an excessively high bar given that many members choose not to participate in strike votes. It considers majority approval by those voting, however, to be acceptable. See International Labour Office (2001).

[30] Workers who participate in general strikes or withhold their labor temporarily to join protests on matters of public interest (e.g., to oppose labor law reforms or to support higher minimum wages) are therefore not legally protected from dismissal.

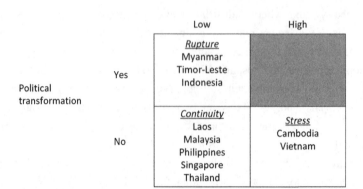

Figure 1 Continuity, rupture, and stress in labor control regimes

in the late 1980s. Such transitions happened in only three countries: Indonesia, Myanmar, and Timor-Leste (see Figure 1). In the remaining countries in the region, regimes were comparatively stable and thus had no reason to transform their labor control regimes, *or* highly unstable, which made profound and enduring labor reforms unlikely. Ruling parties held onto power in Cambodia, Laos, Singapore, and Vietnam. The Philippines remained a highly flawed democracy despite creeping autocratization during Rodrigo Duterte's (2016–22) bloody reign and the election of Ferdinand Marcos's son as president in 2022. Malaysia seemed to be on the verge of democratizing after the opposition PH coalition defeated the BN in the 2018 general election, but less than two years later the government fell. With three governments in the last four years, Malaysian politics are turbulent (Chin 2022). Thailand's politics are the most unsettled in the region, and it has veered between autocracy and democracy since 2006 (McCargo 2021). In these countries, then, there was not a strong impetus to lift existing controls on labor.

By contrast, regime change in a more democratic direction usually results in a lifting of many state controls on the labor movement, and legal reforms were more far reaching in countries that transitioned after the Cold War ended. The relaxation of legal and political controls enables workers to form unions and to participate in democratic life through their unions without constant fear of being arrested for their trade union activities and without intrusive administrative restrictions. In Indonesia, Myanmar, and Timor-Leste, regime change *ruptured* preexisting authoritarian state labor control regimes, which created new opportunities for workers to act collectively through their unions. Governments allowed new and independent unions to gain legal status (Ford 2000; 2016; Gillan and Thein 2016). Unions in all three countries – even the former state-backed union in Indonesia – began to actively defend their members against rights violations, organize strikes, and advocate on public policy issues such as raising the minimum wage (APHEDA 2018; Caraway and Ford 2020; Ford 2016; New Straits Times 2020; Panimbang and Mufakhir 2018). The state's diminished role in disciplining labor also facilitated worker mobilization, especially in Indonesia and Timor-Leste. In Myanmar workers still faced beatings by the police and hired thugs during prolonged strikes, but they nevertheless still engaged frequently in collective action (Arnold and Campbell 2017; Gillan and Thein 2016; Henry 2016).

While political transitions ruptured preexisting labor control regimes, economic transformations *stressed* them. As Kammen (1997) argued in his analysis of Indonesia's strike wave in the early 1990s, the growth of labor-intensive export industries in the late 1980s and early 1990s created challenges for the labor control regime established during import-substituting industrialization. To remain competitive in international markets, employers in exporting sectors needed to control costs. Unable to free themselves from extortion by local officials, the security apparatus, and corrupt unions, employers held down production costs by squeezing workers harder. As working conditions and pay deteriorated, worker grievances mounted. But the actors tasked with containing labor conflict were the same ones that extorted employers. Workers' unresolved grievances created the tinder for the strike wave.[31] This chain of events is especially likely to emerge when labor-intensive export sectors grow rapidly and become major employers, and where high levels of corruption exist.[32]

In the twenty-first century, only two countries – Cambodia and Vietnam – met these conditions (see Table 9). In the rest of the region, industrial employment expanded at a slower pace, did not become a major employer, or contracted. In Laos and Timor-Leste, industrial employment surged but still accounted for a small fraction of total employment; both economies were still dominated by agriculture. In Indonesia, the Philippines, and Thailand, industrial employment grew slowly from a comparatively high baseline, while in Malaysia and Singapore industrial employment contracted. Industry's share of employment expanded only modestly in Myanmar after its political opening in 2011, and agricultural employment still dwarfed industrial employment there.

---

[31] As Kammen argues, these are merely propitious conditions for a strike wave. Export drives in Malaysia, Singapore, and Thailand in the 1970s and 1980s also generated substantial new employment in industry without major strike waves erupting.

[32] This dynamic has similarities to Silver's (2003) "Marxist-type labor unrest" carried out by a newly emerging working class. National-level institutions do not feature prominently in Silver's account, however.

Table 9 Industry's share of employment in Southeast Asia, 2000–19

	Share of employment (%) (2000)	Share of employment (%) (2010)	Share of employment (%) (2019)
Cambodia			
Industry	8.5	16.0	27.9
Agriculture/industry	8.65	3.58	1.24
Indonesia			
Industry	17.4	18.7	22.4
Agriculture/industry	2.6	2.09	1.27
Laos			
Industry	4.6	8.3	12.9
Agriculture/industry	17.8	8.61	4.76
Malaysia			
Industry	32.2	27.6	27.0
Agriculture/industry	0.57	0.48	0.38
Myanmar			
Industry	12.9	16.5	16.9
Agriculture/industry	4.74	3.22	2.89
Philippines			
Industry	15.9	15.7	19.1
Agriculture/industry	2.33	2.1	1.2
Singapore			
Industry	28.0	21.9	15.6
Agriculture/industry	0.01	0.0	0.0
Thailand			
Industry	19.0	20.6	22.8
Agriculture/industry	2.57	1.86	1.38
Timor-Leste			
Industry	8.7	9.3	16.3
Agriculture/industry	6.68	5.46	2.41
Vietnam			
Industry	12.4	21.7	27.4
Agriculture/industry	5.27	2.24	1.36

Source: World Bank, World Development Indicators

By contrast, industrial employment grew rapidly *and* came to comprise a significant share of total employment in Cambodia and Vietnam. Export-oriented and labor-intensive sectors spurred this expansion in industrial employment in both countries (Vogiatzoglou 2019). The brisk growth in industrial employment combined with high levels of corruption strained systems of labor control.[33] Employers squeezed workers to maintain their edge on global markets, while governments were loath to raise minimum wages substantially for fear that doing so would drive away investment. In both countries, the real value of the minimum wage declined dramatically in the first decade of the century and did not cover basic needs (Labour Behind the Label and Cambodian Legal Education Centre 2013; Tran 2012). Wildcat strikes skyrocketed in both countries (Do 2017; Tek 2022).

In the countries that experienced neither enduring regime change nor industrial transformation – Laos, Malaysia, the Philippines, Singapore, and Thailand – labor contention was minimal. Labor control regimes from the late twentieth century have remained intact, and strike action in each of these countries continued to be rare. Workers in Laos seldom strike (Fry and Mees 2016), while in Singapore, there has been a single strike in the last decade, and in Malaysia, none have occurred.[34] Between 2015 and 2019, there were on average only five strikes per year in Thailand and about ten per year in the Philippines from 2011 to 2019.[35]

3.4 Conclusion

The situation of organized labor in Southeast Asia in the twenty-first century in many ways mirrors that of the final decades of the previous century. Historical legacies, regime persistence, and the timing of democratization and political openings explain these continuities. However, the twenty-first century has not merely reproduced past patterns. In countries that democratized or liberalized, or that experienced an explosion of employment in labor-intensive export industries, old methods of labor control ruptured or came under stress, and workers became more contentious. This occurred not only in democracies but also in autocracies and hybrid regimes. The next section delves more deeply into the anatomies of contention in the three countries with the highest level of worker mobilization: Cambodia, Indonesia, and Vietnam.

4 Anatomies of Contention: Cambodia, Indonesia, and Vietnam

Workers in Cambodia, Indonesia, and Vietnam have been the most contentious in Southeast Asia in recent years. They frequently strike and to varying extents also

---

[33] In 2021, Transparency International scored Cambodia 23 and Vietnam 39 on its Corruption Perceptions Index. The scale ranges from zero (highly corrupt) to 100 (very clean). Out of 180 countries, ordered from least corrupt to most corrupt, Vietnam placed 87th and Cambodia 157th. See www.transparency.org/en/cpi/2021.

[34] ILO, Industrial Relations Dataset which is accessible via https://ilostat.ilo.org/, and Malaysia's Department of Human Resources statistics (https://jpp.mohr.gov.my/sumber/statistik-portal).

[35] ILO, Industrial Relations Dataset.

make collective demands to governments on policy matters affecting workers. Only one of these countries – Indonesia – is a democracy. Although there is no correlation between regime type and labor contentiousness, it does have consequences for the shape that worker protest assumes, and the extent to which unions are the mobilizing agents. I link these different anatomies of contention to regime context and the structure of the trade union landscape. Each case study outlines the distinctive features of each country's anatomy of contention, focusing analytically on the form that worker mobilization takes and on government responses to it.

4.1 Patterns of Contention: Worker-Led versus Union-Led

Although workers in Cambodia, Indonesia, and Vietnam frequently engage in collective action, the form that it takes varies. In some countries, unions are the primary agent organizing worker mobilization, while in others, unions play a less prominent role. This pattern of contention is related to regime type and the presence or absence of independent unions.

In terms of regime type, the three countries run the gamut from full-fledged autocracy to democracy. Cambodia was a competitive authoritarian regime until 2017. There, opposition parties vigorously contested but always lost elections to Hun Sen's CPP. Despite rampant violations of civil liberties, an increasingly robust civil society comprising non-governmental organizations, community groups, and labor unions also developed (Un 2019). In Vietnam, the VCP has ruled since reunification in 1975 and has not permitted opposition parties to contest elections.[36] There are no legal channels for challenging the party's monopoly, and civil society organizations are more constrained than in Cambodia (Landau 2008). Finally, Indonesia was a democracy during this period, with highly competitive elections and a vibrant civil society (Davidson 2018; Mietzner 2012). With few exceptions, autonomous groups could organize freely, criticize government policies, and express their discontent in public protests without fear of violent retribution.

These differences in regime context, in turn, had consequences for the structuring of each country's trade unions. In Vietnam, there is only one union, the VGCL that is organically linked but subordinate to the VCP (Hansson 2003). In Cambodia, although a significant proportion of Cambodia's many union federations are closely aligned with the ruling CPP, independent unions exist as well (Nuon and Serrano 2010). Indonesia, like Cambodia, also has a dizzying number of unions, but none of them are organically tied to a political party (Caraway and Ford 2020).

---

[36] In Vietnam, candidates for elected office are nominated by the party, the military, and state agencies. Independent self-nominations are also permitted (Truong 2021).

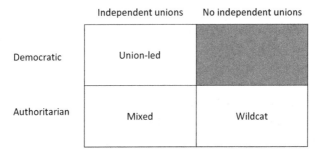

Figure 2 Dominant patterns of labor contention

This combination of regime type and union landscape combine to produce distinct patterns of worker contention. Although workers frequently protest and strike in all three countries, the primary mode through which they express their discontent varies (see Figure 2). In Vietnam, protest is predominantly *worker-led* and wildcat in nature.[37] Even when the VGCL is present, workers act without its encouragement. Because unions are not leading these strikes, they are usually "spontaneous," that is, minimal advanced planning occurs, and workers do not follow the required process for mounting a legal strike. These wildcat actions typically take place at or near the place of work and are apolitical in that they are not linked to outside groups and do not challenge the VCP (Buckley 2021b; Kerkvliet 2010; Tran 2007b).

At the other end of the spectrum from Vietnam is Indonesia, where the dominant pattern of worker protest is *union-led*. Of course, Indonesian workers who do not belong to unions, and even some who are unionized, do act autonomously from unions. But where unions are present, they are typically involved with planning and coordinating collective action, whether it be in the workplace or the public sphere. Unions engage in both strikes targeted at specific employers and larger actions that bring workers from many unions and workplaces together in the streets to make collective demands to local and national governments (Caraway and Ford 2020).

---

[37] I follow Anner (2015) in linking the wildcat worker-led mode of protest in Vietnam to the authoritarian state labor control regime. Buckley (2021b) contests this claim, arguing that the informalization of formal sector work is the driving force. When formal sector jobs become ever more precarious, he argues, workers engage in decentralized resistance such as wildcat strikes. However, the informalization of formal sector work is happening around the region and produces different patterns of labor contention, with unions playing a prominent role in some countries and not in others. While I concur with Anner regarding Vietnam, I do not find that international accords – transnational agreements negotiated between unions and multinational corporations to hold lead firms accountable for conditions in their supplier factories – are the primary form of worker resistance in despotic market regimes. Although unions in Cambodia and Indonesia have pressured international buyers to bolster their bargaining position, wildcat actions, union-led strikes, and public protests are more prominent than international accords.

In Cambodia, the combination of independent and regime-backed unions produces a *mixed* pattern of worker protest in which there is a more even balance between union-led and worker-led mobilization. Unlike the VGCL, Cambodia's regime-linked unions do not have a monopoly of representation and thus risk losing members to other unions if they do not advocate for them when disputes arise (Nuon and Serrano 2010; Oka 2016). Both independent and regime-sponsored unions may therefore organize strikes when employers refuse to address workers' concerns. But workers also commonly engage in wildcat actions, even in unionized workplaces (Tek 2022; Ward and Mouyly 2016). In addition to strikes, independent unions also organize protests that unite workers from different factories behind policy concerns such as the minimum wage. Regime-linked unions, however, seldom join these public rallies that directly confront the government.

Government and employer responses to worker contention have also varied considerably across these three countries. In Indonesia and Vietnam, governments have rarely cracked down harshly on worker protests. Striking workers face few negative consequences for taking industrial action in Vietnam, where state authorities typically side with workers and prod employers to make concessions (Clarke 2006; Kerkvliet 2010). In Indonesia, although employers commonly fired striking workers and/or strike leaders, local and national governments seldom responded violently to strikes or to large protests around issues such as minimum wages and labor regulations (Caraway 2013, 2010; Caraway and Ford 2020). When protestors became unruly – for example, tearing down gates around government offices – police might respond with targeted arrests, water cannons, and/or tear gas. But these responses were both measured and rare before Joko Widodo became president in 2014.[38] By contrast, Cambodia's government has cracked down harshly on worker protests, resulting in numerous fatalities and injuries. Extrajudicial executions, arrests, and legal harassment have also occurred (Ford et al. 2021; Hall 2010; Hughes 2007).

While workers in these countries share a proclivity for protest, then, there are important differences in the shape that their actions take, the involvement of unions in mobilizing workers, and state responses to their actions. The next three sections provide a more detailed analysis of these varying anatomies of contention as well as a discussion of the backlash against organized labor in Cambodia and Indonesia since 2014 and recent labor reforms in Vietnam.

4.2 Anatomies of Contention I: Vietnam

In Vietnam, the primary form of worker contention is wildcat strikes organized at the grassroots by workers themselves, without the assistance of unions. Such

---

[38] For some important exceptions, see Caraway (2010).

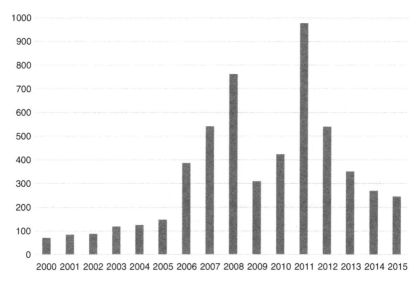

Figure 3 Strikes in Vietnam, 2000–15
Source: Tran et al. (2017), based on VGCL-collected data.

strikes have become a routine feature of the industrial relations landscape, and increasingly so over the course of the twenty-first century (see Figure 3). In the early 2000s, there were fewer than 100 strikes per year, but since 2006 there have never been fewer than 200 strikes per year, peaking in 2011 when nearly 1,000 strikes occurred.[39] The majority of strikes erupted in foreign-owned businesses that produced for export and were typically unrelated to collective bargaining negotiations (Do 2017; Tran 2007b). Workers' demands initially focused on compliance with labor laws, but they increasingly sought pay and working conditions above and beyond legal requirements (Lee 2006).

Surprisingly, given that the VGCL is present in many workplaces, there is no record of the union ever leading a strike (Clarke 2006; Kerkvliet 2010; Lee 2006; Siu and Chan 2015).[40] Since upper-level trade union officials usually negotiate the union's entry into a workplace directly with management rather than through organizing workers at the grassroots, the VGCL's company-level leadership is often ill-equipped or disinclined to advocate for workers (Clarke 2006; Do 2017; Schweisshelm and Chi 2018; Tran 2007a). Workers therefore

---

[39] Clarke (2006) argues that these data likely underestimate the actual number of strikes because many work stoppages are brief and are resolved quickly and hence do not appear in VGCL statistics.

[40] Do (2017) reports that in some cases, enterprise level union leaders covertly support strikes after negotiations with management fail to resolve disputes. Then, once the strike breaks out, they negotiate an end to the strike.

often take matters into their own hands by downing tools. Although these strikes are "leaderless" in that there is no union organizing them, they are usually well organized, with high levels of solidarity (Clarke 2006; Do 2017; Lee 2006; Kerkvliet 2010; Siu and Chan 2015). Strike waves are also common. When workers with strong informal organization wrest a wage increase from employers, workers in neighboring companies often go out on strike as well (Clarke 2006; Do 2017). Workers also learn about strikes at other factories through newspaper accounts that often portray worker demands sympathetically, inspiring workers in other workplaces to take similar action (Tran 2007b).

Although the VGCL does not organize strikes, leaders at higher levels of the union play a vital role in resolving disputes once a strike breaks out. Some scholars have found evidence that work stoppages are more common in unionized enterprises, possibly because workers anticipate that the union will step in quickly on their behalf (Anner and Liu 2016; Do 2017). When strikes occur, local authorities dispatch ad hoc teams of VGCL and state officials to resolve the conflict quickly (Clarke 2006). Even though these strikes do not follow the prescribed legal procedures, strike ringleaders are seldom punished, and the authorities often pressure employers to make concessions (Clarke 2006; Lee 2006; Kerkvliet 2010; Schweisshelm and Chi 2018; Siu and Chan 2015). Since unions typically intervene to help resolve conflicts in workers' favor, it is not surprising that despite the top-down nature of the VGCL, surveys show that a majority of workers believe that unions represent their interests (Siu and Chan 2015). Trade union leaders and party officials have consistently demonstrated sympathy for nonviolent strikers at the enterprise level, both in words and deeds, and have openly blamed employers for provoking strikes by violating labor law (Anner and Liu 2016, 6; Siu and Chan 2015). The VCP tolerates the proliferation of strikes in part because they are usually peaceful, with modest demands that do not challenge its authority. Unlike Cambodia and Indonesia, the Vietnamese government has not used COVID-19 restrictions as a pretext to crack down on worker protest (Buckley 2020; Ford and Ward 2021).

As in many other countries in the region, Vietnam's workers have also increasingly taken up the issue of minimum wages, which are an urgent concern because in the absence of strong collective bargaining institutions they are the effective wage for formal sector workers (Clarke 2006). Contention takes a different form than in Cambodia and Indonesia, however. Whereas Cambodian and Indonesian workers organize protests in public space that bring workers from different workplaces together in the streets, Vietnam's workers conduct strikes at the factories where they work. Even though the government, not employers, sets the minimum wage, workers do not explicitly direct their protests at the government as this would likely provoke a sterner response.

Worker dissatisfaction over the minimum wage drove the first major strike wave in December 2005–January 2006. The government had not raised the minimum wage for a decade, and inflation had significantly eroded its purchasing power (Clarke 2006; Tran 2007b). At the time, the government was aware that the real decline in wages could prompt conflict, and it signaled that a minimum wage increase was on the horizon. Beginning in September 2005, press reports tantalized workers with the prospect of a big raise in 2006. But the government wavered about the size and the timing of the increase. In the meantime, the first wave of strikes demanding higher wages broke out in the last days of December 2005 (Clarke 2006). In response, the prime minister soon announced a 40 percent increase in the minimum wage in the foreign sector. Employers begged for mercy, so the government delayed implementation until after Tet. This postponement invited yet another wave of strikes in which workers insisted that employers begin paying the higher wage immediately. Workers in domestic enterprises also struck because the government had only increased the minimum wage in the foreign-owned sector (Clarke 2006). In all, tens of thousands of workers participated, and employers soon capitulated to workers' demands in order to get production back online (Clarke 2006, 359; Clarke et al. 2007; Tran 2007b).

After this strike wave, the government began to adjust minimum wages annually to preempt future turmoil over wages. But despite annual minimum wage hikes, workers continued to strike in large numbers as spiraling inflation ate away at their wages (Siu and Chan 2015). Although the government raised the minimum wage to adjust for inflation, strikes did not abate because many foreign-owned factories did not pay the higher wage and the minimum wage continued to be well below a living wage (Siu and Chan 2015; Tran et al. 2017). Most strikes continued to center on wages and working conditions, but in 2015 workers at the Pou Yuen factory and twenty-seven other companies in Ho Chi Minh City also staged wildcat strikes over a change to the national government's pension policy.[41] The National Assembly acceded to the workers' demands by passing a resolution amending the law (Chan and Hui 2022).

In Vietnam, the combination of enterprise unions that are weak and unrepresentative, low wages, and the government's rapid and sympathetic responses to strikes, have produced an impressive surge in worker-led strikes. Given that the minimum

---

[41] The amendment required workers to wait until retirement to collect a lump sum payment. Previously, workers could collect it upon termination of employment. In 2003, workers struck over this issue as well, and the government also reversed course (Chan and Hui 2022).

wage is far below a living wage, it would be incorrect to claim that the government is pro-worker. But in contrast to Cambodia and Indonesia, there has not been a regime backlash against labor. Instead, the regime is testing softer methods to rein in worker militancy. In January 2021, a new Labor Code went into effect that allows workers to form independent worker representative organizations (WROs) at the enterprise level. WROs are not required to affiliate to the VGCL. They can bargain collectively and organize strikes but cannot form higher-level organizations. While some scholars attribute this reform to trade agreements (Tran et al. 2017), Buckley (2021a) persuasively argues that the main impetus is the desire to stem the tide of wildcat strikes by building "harmonious labor relations" at the plant level. The VGCL has obviously failed in this task, in part because of its weak ties to workers. Whether workers are keen to establish WROs, however, remains an open question. Downing tools produces concessions, and quickly, so the benefit of WROs may not be immediately apparent to workers.

4.3 Anatomies of Contention II: Indonesia

As in Vietnam, Indonesian workers also frequently strike (see Figure 4), but in Indonesia, unions play a central role in organizing them. With dozens of independent federations and numerous unaffiliated unions, competition for members impels unions at the enterprise level to be attentive to workers' concerns. Unions commonly negotiate with employers to settle disputes and lead strikes when these negotiations fail.[42] Many workplaces are not unionized, and workers there also carry out wildcat actions. Even many strikes led by unions are deemed by courts to be illegal because unions have deviated from the legal requirements for striking or because courts have inconsistently interpreted the requirements for mounting legal strikes (Caraway 2013).

Although in the decade or so after democratization, most worker contention was centered in workplaces, over time it increasingly occurred in public space – for example, in front of government buildings and parliament, on toll roads (Panimbang and Mufakhir 2018). By 2012, only about 38 percent of protests occurred in industrial estates or workplaces, and in 37 percent of all protests that year, workers' demands focused on policy change (Panimbang and Mufakhir 2018, 24–25). Even in the early transition years, however, unions turned out their members on the streets to resist labor reforms that unions opposed, and these large protests usually resulted in substantial concessions to workers' demands (Caraway Forthcoming a; Caraway and Ford 2020). But it was the fierce contention around minimum wages that produced

---

[42] It is also not uncommon for unions to strike first (*aksi dulu*), then negotiate because they think that employers will not negotiate seriously unless workers first demonstrate their resolve.

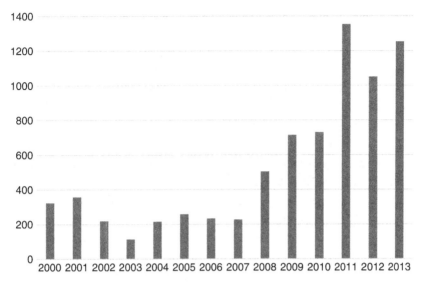

Figure 4 Strikes in Indonesia, 2000–13

Source: Panimbang and Mufakhir (2018). Data do not include May Day celebrations or the general strikes in 2012 and 2013.

the crescendo of worker protest in 2011–13 and a shift of worker contention from the workplace to the streets.

From 2003 until 2010, minimum wages had increased roughly in line with inflation, but these incremental increases still fell short of the government-defined decent living standard, which was the legal benchmark for the minimum wage (Caraway et al. 2019). The system for setting minimum wages was highly decentralized in Indonesia. In industrial areas, elected local executives made wage recommendations annually to governors, in consultation with tripartite wage councils. Beginning in 2010, local networks of unions, with assistance from national federations, began to organize more deliberately around the annual minimum wage negotiations (Caraway et al. 2019; Panimbang and Mufakhir 2018; Tjandra 2016). These local networks united many different unions. They coordinated negotiating strategies and dispatched members to protest in front of local government offices during key moments of the wage negotiations. The most intense mobilizations happened in the 2011–12 wage cycle. Workers rioted in the industrial center of Batam, shutting down the city for two days. In Bekasi and Tangerang, workers repeatedly paralyzed industrial zones and toll roads in the Jakarta metropolitan area. The response of both local and national governments was capitulation: minimum wages rose substantially that year, and the national government threw its weight behind more robust future increases. Unions built on this momentum with an impressive national strike in 2012, strategically timed to influence minimum wage negotiations that were ongoing across the country. The result was unprecedented wage increases in industrial areas. This combination of semi-institutionalized local union networks and national organizations that have, on occasion, effectively coordinated action across the country and in Jakarta, sets Indonesia apart from Cambodia and Vietnam. This ability to mobilize large numbers of workers in public space has also allowed unions to take on a more prominent role in electoral politics, running numerous candidates for major political parties in local and national races, fielding candidates for district head, and endorsing candidates for district head, mayor, governor, and president (Caraway and Ford 2014; Caraway, Ford et al. 2015)

The most militant union campaign was the factory raids in May–October 2012, during which workers in Bekasi took over at least one hundred factories (Mufakhir 2014). Labor activists identified factories where employers used outsourced labor in violation of the law, and if management refused to end illegal practices, workers immediately struck. Unions then sent instructions through their networks calling on members to report to the factory to support the raid. Although these actions resulted in thousands of temporary workers being made permanent, they also prompted employers to recruit local thugs and community leaders to harass workers participating in the raids. The local government stood by as attacks on workers escalated, and the factory raids soon came to an end.

This counterattack in Bekasi was a foretaste of a vigorous backlash against labor under the presidency of Joko Widodo (better known as Jokowi) (2014–24).[43] Early in his first term, he issued Government Regulation no. 78/2015 on Wages, better known as PP78, to address employer complaints about surging minimum wages. PP78 required local wage councils to set minimum wages according to a national formula rather than through negotiations, thereby transforming the wage councils into rubber stamp bodies. Wage increases fell dramatically, especially in the industrial and metropolitan areas where unions were strongest (Caraway et al. 2019). The next major blow came in Jokowi's second term, with the passage of Law No. 11/2020 on Job Creation, or the Omnibus Law, in October 2020. This law included a slew of amendments to the Manpower Act that fulfilled longstanding employer demands for greater labor flexibility.[44]

---

[43] The rest of this section draws on Caraway (Forthcoming a).

[44] The most far-reaching changes in the law included the following: the decent living standard was no longer the benchmark for minimum wages, small enterprises became exempt from paying the minimum wage, sectoral minimum wages were eliminated, severance pay was reduced, restrictions on the length of time that workers could be employed on fixed term contracts and the types of work that could be outsourced were removed, overtime limits were raised from three to four

Unions turned out in the streets, as they had done under previous administrations, but under Jokowi their actions did not bear fruit and produced the harshest measures against labor since the Suharto years. Although Indonesia is still categorized as a competitive electoral democracy, democratic recession accelerated under Jokowi. His administration has used more aggressive tactics than his predecessors to attack political opponents inside and outside of government (Aspinall and Mietzner 2019). For example, when more than 10,000 workers assembled peacefully outside the presidential palace to demand that the president revoke PP78, the police beat protestors, forcibly dispersed them with water cannons and tear gas, and arrested twenty-five people (Mufakhir and Pelu 2015). The following month, police arrested forty-two protestors in several cities. The police began to strictly enforce a national law that prohibited demonstrations close to "vital" installations such as the presidential palace and increased the number of industrial parks and corporations classified as vital, giving the security apparatus wider powers to legally shut down and preempt protests. They also blocked key arteries leading into Jakarta to prevent workers from the industrial suburbs around the capital from flooding Jakarta with protestors, intensified surveillance of unions, and selectively harassed some of the most vocal labor leaders. Once the pandemic broke out in 2020, the authorities used restrictions on public gatherings to prohibit protests and to limit their size. In the run-up to the parliamentary session for approving the Omnibus Law, for example, the national police issued a letter instructing officers not to grant permission for rallies, citing concerns about COVID-19 spreading.[45] After the bill became law, clashes with police were reported in at least a dozen cities, resulting in several deaths and hundreds of arrests. Although labor remains highly contentious in Indonesia, workers had to scale back their protests during the pandemic and are still reeling from the dramatic reversal of fortune under Jokowi.

4.4 Anatomies of Contention III: Cambodia

As in Indonesia, Cambodia's unions also organize work stoppages and protests that bring together workers from different workplaces in the streets. But wildcat actions are also common, even when unions are present in the workplace. Most union members toil in the apparel industry, which has accounted for 70–80 percent of the nation's exports (Asuyama and Neou 2014; Nuon and Serrano 2010). About 60 percent of workers in this sector belong to a union, and in many

---

hours per day and from fourteen to eighteen hours per week, and workers lost their right to long-service leave.

[45] Another damper on protest was that employers, citing the national law on quarantines, required workers who participated in protests to quarantine, without pay, for fourteen days.

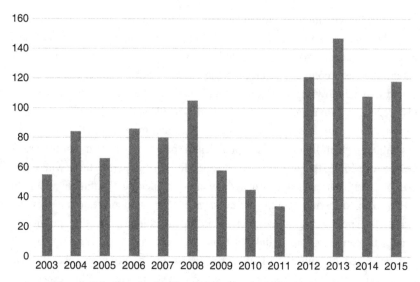

Figure 5 Strikes in the Cambodian garment industry, 2003–15
Source: Garment Manufacturing Association of Cambodia (GMAC).

workplaces multiple unions are present (Nuon and Serrano 2010). As can be seen in Figure 5, workers in the apparel industry are avid strikers.[46]

Unions of all political persuasions organize strikes. Regime-backed unions may not confront the government directly, but if they do not attend to workers' grievances in the workplace, they risk losing members to other unions. If one union ignores their concerns, workers shop around for another one that is more attentive. Plant-level unions play a central role in resolving disputes, and when these efforts fail, unions may initiate strike action in consultation with federation leadership (Lawreniuk 2020; Oka 2016). Although workers frequently channel their demands through unions when they are present in the workplace, workers also engage in wildcat actions to redress urgent grievances (Arnold 2017; Doutch 2021). Lengthy strike authorization procedures and dispute resolution processes, and the nonbinding nature of most Arbitration Council rulings, conspire to delay redress, prompting workers to take matters into their own hands.[47] Even unions seldom adhere to the lengthy procedures for

---

[46] These data undercount actual strike activity as they do not include other sectors or protests that occur outside the workplace. Individual-level survey data also reveal high strike propensity among Cambodian workers. In a survey of 291 workers in three Hong Kong-owned factories in Phnom Penh, Franceschini (2020) found that more than half of respondents admitted to participating in a strike and 66.5 percent agreed that strikes were a legitimate means for protecting worker rights and interests.

[47] Tek (2022) argues that strikes serve as an alternative enforcement mechanism in countries with weak rule of law. Weak enforcement of labor laws, drawn-out dispute resolution procedures, and employer noncompliance with arbitration rulings, she argues, drove workers to disrupt

mounting a legal strike (Better Factories Cambodia 2018, 2009; Nuon and Serrano 2010; Tek 2022). In addition to work stoppages that aim to wrest concessions from employers, independent unions also mobilize workers on issues of shared concern such as the minimum wage. These protests occur in public space and workers direct their demands to the government. Government responses to strikes and protests have been comparatively harsh, and seem to be especially vicious in the runup to and aftermath of close elections. The assassination of two prominent leaders of independent unions in the wake of the 2003 election, is the most shocking example, but violence and intimidation – both legal and physical, and by both employers and the state – are an endemic feature of Cambodia's labor relations (Arnold 2013; Hall 2010; Worker Rights Consortium 2014). Independent unions' strong international contacts and Cambodia's dependence on garment exports have checked but not ended these abuses.

Worker protests around minimum wages illustrate well the pattern of high mobilization and state suppression of worker militancy. Starting in 2010, demonstrations focusing on the minimum wage became bigger and bolder. Minimum wages were an urgent issue for Cambodian workers. In the absence of robust collective bargaining institutions, workers only received a raise if the government agreed to increase the minimum wage. Between 2001 and 2011, real minimum wages in the garment industry fell 19.1 percent and were so low that many workers suffered from malnutrition (Worker Rights Consortium 2014). To address this parlous situation, unions on the tripartite panel that made wage recommendations to the government agreed to advocate for a $93 minimum wage in 2010 – a 66 percent raise. The government endorsed a much lower increase – $56 and $61 for fixed duration and unlimited duration workers – prompting independent unions to organize a four-day national strike in which tens of thousands of workers participated. The government refused to revisit the minimum wage until 2014, however, and both the government and employers took legal action against strike leaders. Many striking workers were also suspended or fired (Arnold 2013).

Predictably, government inaction on the minimum wage set the stage for even larger protests in 2013–14. Minimum wages remained far below what even government-sponsored bodies concluded were necessary for workers to live decently – $160 – but the minimum wage proposed on December 24 fell far short at $80. Even though this was the highest increase in more than a decade – over 30 percent – several unions expressed their dismay and demanded a more

---

production to force employers to comply with the law. This tactic can be extremely effective in the garment industry because the international buyers set tight production deadlines and impose penalties when suppliers fail to meet them.

generous raise. But it was workers at the grassroots, not unions, that initiated the worker revolt in late December and early January. Significantly, participants included not only members of independent unions, but also nonunionized workers and members of pro-government unions. In response to these wildcat actions, employers locked out workers, further enflaming the situation and resulting in even more workers taking to the streets. For a week, workers occupied the center of Phnom Penh, blocking roads around the Ministry of Labor. Protests peaked on December 29, the same day as a large rally by the largest opposition party, the Cambodian National Rescue Party (CNRP). This time worker protests bore fruit. On December 31, the Ministry of Labor announced that the minimum wage would be increased to $100 effective February 1. But this concession was insufficient to quell the protests, and ultimately the police suppressed the strikers, resulting in five deaths, and dozens of injuries and arrests (Asia Monitor Resource Centre et al. 2014; Worker Rights Consortium 2014).

As in Indonesia, worker militancy invited a backlash against organized labor. The opposition CNRP performed surprisingly well in garment-intensive electoral districts in the 2013 elections, thanks in part to union support. The crackdown on independent unions was therefore part of a broader attack on opposition forces after the 2013 national election (Ford et al. Forthcoming; Salmivaara 2018). Employers dismissed at least 867 union leaders and workers for joining a union or participating in labor protests (International Labour Office 2017b). The regime also charged many trade union leaders and activists with criminal offenses related to their union activities, and injunctions and requisition orders against unions and workers engaged in industrial actions increased as well (International Labour Office 2017a). In addition to these overtly coercive measures, the regime also deployed more subtle means to rein in independent unions (Ford et al. Forthcoming; Lawreniuk Forthcoming). As the regime criminalized labor activists, it also enacted a new Trade Union Law in 2016 that required voting members, candidates for union office, and union leaders to sign a declaration that they had never been convicted of a criminal offense. The law put in place more elaborate registration procedures that gave the state apparatus new legal tools to torment unions and granted the courts expansive powers to dissolve unions. It also stipulated that only the most representative union could bring cases to the widely respected Arbitration Council.[48]

---

[48] Unions must dedicate significant time and effort to prove that they are the most representative union, and those that gain this status often do so by colluding with the employer. The number of cases brought to the Arbitration Council declined precipitously after 2016 (Lawreniuk Forthcoming).

The authorities have also deployed the State of Emergency law declared in response to the COVID-19 pandemic to limit protests (Ford and Ward 2021).

This onslaught against independent unions had obvious implications for union involvement in organizing worker protest. With so many union leaders tied up in court or preoccupied with filing paperwork to maintain their legal status, union capacity was strained. In addition, the constant threat of legal retaliation for organizing strikes raised the costs for the unions and leaders that organized them. This, combined with the CPP's efforts to placate workers with regular minimum wage increases and various financial incentives at election time, resulted in a substantial decline in demonstrations starting in 2017 (Bynum and Pfadt 2019; Ford et al. Forthcoming).[49] This strategy, however, may backfire. As the regime debilitates independent unions, workers will increasingly have to act on their own, which may very well lead to a resurgence of the labor strife that it sought to squelch in the first place (Lawreniuk Forthcoming).

4.5 Conclusion

Workers in Cambodia, Indonesia, and Vietnam have been the most contentious in the region in the first two decades of the twenty-first century. Although they are similar in their feistiness, each country has a distinctive anatomy of contention. These varying anatomies of contention are in turn linked to regime type – whether a country is democratic or not – and the presence of independent unions. In autocracies where independent unions are not present, the dominant form of labor contention is likely to be wildcat in nature, as in Vietnam, but where independent unions exist, as in Cambodia, unions play an important role in organizing strikes and protests. The lone democracy among the three countries, Indonesia, is also the country where unions play the most prominent role in leading and coordinating working class contention.

For much of this period, governments in Indonesia and Vietnam usually responded favorably to protests and rarely suppressed unions or punished activists. In Cambodia, the regime has always shown a greater willingness to crack down on worker mobilization. Since 2014, both the Hun Sen regime in Cambodia and the Jokowi administration in Indonesia began to take more deliberate measures to contain labor. These actions unfolded as part of a broader process of autocratization that entailed clamping down on opposition forces in society. Then the pandemic struck, and in the economic crash that ensued, thousands of workers were laid off. Unions in all three countries have

---

[49] Between 1998 and 2013, the government had raised the minimum wage only three times, but it did so seven times from 2013 to 2020 (Lawreniuk 2020).

advocated for their members during this crisis, but in tandem with government aid programs to support worker incomes during the pandemic, the Hun Sen regime and Jokowi administrations have also used the pandemic to further narrow the political space for labor mobilization (Ford and Ward 2021). Thus, while organized labor in Cambodia and Indonesia was arguably at its peak strength at the beginning of the second decade of the twenty-first century, its position has become increasingly precarious and uncertain as Southeast Asia enters the 2020s.

5 Conclusion

This Element presented an analytic overview of organized labor in Southeast Asia from the end of World War II to the present and offers insight into why labor has not figured more prominently in scholarship of contemporary politics in the region. One reason for this neglect is the organizational weakness of unions and their low levels of mobilization over long stretches of time. The roots of labor's weakness can be traced to the immediate postwar period when Southeast Asia became a major front in the Cold War. Western powers and Southeast Asian ruling classes colluded in rolling back ascendant leftist forces and succeeded in this effort in Indonesia, Malaysia, the Philippines, Singapore, and Thailand. In these countries, ruling classes embraced a capitalist path of accumulation and erected labor control regimes that largely prevented militant labor organizations from re-emerging. Where the postwar rollback project failed, socialist parties eventually came to power, but political turmoil and failed development policies left their economies overwhelmingly dominated by agriculture. Party-linked unions absorbed and contained the tiny industrial working class. Thus, at the end of the twentieth century, organized labor in Southeast Asia was too weak to make much of a mark on politics in the region.

These legacies continue to shape organized labor in the twenty-first century. Despite democratization and political liberalization in several countries, organized labor in Southeast Asia continues to sit on the sidelines in much of the region. Unionization rates remain low, collective bargaining institutions underdeveloped, and serious labor rights violations persist. In some cases, such as the Philippines and Cambodia, these violations are extreme and have resulted in labor activists being gravely injured and killed. Organized labor continues to be contained in much of the region, but workers have shown renewed feistiness in the countries that underwent the most dramatic economic and political transformations. Workers in Cambodia, Indonesia, and Vietnam have been the most contentious in the region, and each has its own characteristic anatomy of contention.

Autocratization, however, has taken a toll on workers' movements and other civil society groups in countries where organized labor was showing new signs of life. This study demonstrates that while working-class movements have not necessarily gained ground in democratic settings, authoritarian regimes have been far more assertive in their efforts to repress and contain organized labor than democracies. Even in Vietnam, worker militance has been tolerated precisely because it is wildcat in nature and has been targeted primarily at employers and not the regime. Thus, the wave of autocratization unfolding in Southeast Asia – in Cambodia, Indonesia, Thailand, the Philippines, and most recently, Myanmar – brings with it renewed challenges for organized labor. Despite the threat that autocratization poses to organized labor, they have only pushed back assertively in one country: Myanmar. The weak resistance in countries where unions have not shown much mobilizational capacity in recent years – the Philippines and Thailand – is hardly surprising. But organized labor's feeble response is more surprising in countries where unions were more militant.

In an astute analysis of democratic backsliding in the Philippines and Thailand, Thompson (2021) has linked the forcefulness of civil society pushback against democratic regression to the electoral legitimacy of those attacking democratic practices. Where there is widespread sentiment that autocratizing leaders have no electoral legitimacy – for example, because they rigged an election or overthrew an elected government – civil society groups are more easily catalyzed into a broad-based defense of democracy. But where elected leaders can claim that they have won office through legitimate democratic elections, such broad-based resistance is less likely. In line with Thompson's analysis, the two countries where militaries overthrew elected governments – Myanmar and Thailand – significant civil society pushback occurred. But it was only in Myanmar that worker organizations joined forces with other civil society groups in the streets.

This vigorous response is due in large part to a quick recognition of the threat. Decades of repression under military rule meant that Myanmar's workers were well aware of its dire consequences for unions (Haack and Hlaing 2021).[50] Although organized labor had its grievances with the NLD, there was no doubt that the military would be far worse (Levenson 2021). Thus, in the early days after the coup, women-led garment unions from the industrial areas surrounding Yangon played a pivotal role in mobilizing thousands of workers to join protests in the city center (Jordt et al. 2021). By the end of the month, unions began to coordinate with other civil society groups and nonunionized workers to carry out a rolling general strike that paralyzed Myanmar's economy and state

---

[50] The next three paragraphs draw on Caraway (Forthcoming b).

bureaucracy (Anonymous 2021; Haack and Hlaing 2021; Schrank 2021). During the bloody crackdown on the resistance, the military government declared sixteen labor organizations to be illegal and arrested prominent union leaders (Connell 2021). The military remains in power today and shows no sign of ceding power to civilians or of lifting restrictions on unions.

In Indonesia, by contrast, organized labor and civil society were slow to understand the threat. Polarization between supporters of Jokowi and Prabowo undoubtedly contributed to weak pushback (Mietzner 2021). But perhaps just as important is the slow-moving nature of democratic recession, which dulled labor's and other civil society groups' response to the erosion of democratic freedoms. Like a frog in water that slowly comes to a boil, unions did not realize that the measures deployed against them during Jokowi's first term were part of an incremental process of executive aggrandizement that targeted not only labor but all opposition to his government. Many unions saw Jokowi as a mere stooge for business because of his anti-labor policies, not as a threat to democracy. All unions, including those that had supported Jokowi's candidacy in 2014 and 2019, turned out their members to oppose his anti-labor policies. But they did not protest measures that directly attacked institutions of accountability, Islamists, opposition parties, or regime critics. It wasn't until his second term, after the passage of the Omnibus Law, that union leaders began to understand that Jokowi's anti-labor agenda was part of a broader attack on liberal democracy (Caraway Forthcoming a). By then, COVID-19 provided a public health justification for repressing anti-government protest, and the government savvily used divide-and-rule tactics to dull labor's response. Southeast Asia's strongest labor movement has thus not pushed back very effectively against democracy's erosion.[51]

The incremental pace of autocratization also dulled organized labor's response in Cambodia. Unlike in Indonesia, the leaders of independent unions understood early on that autocratization was underway and presented a threat to their continued existence. On the other hand, incrementalism allowed Hun Sen to deploy divide-and-rule tactics that disorganized civil society and the opposition, leaving each group flailing to protect itself. The suppression of the 2013–14 protests had resulted in numerous fatalities and injuries, and before independent unions had

---

[51] However, there are signs that some prominent union leaders now understand the threat and are taking a firmer stand. In February 2022, Jokowi supporters began lobbying for a postponement of the 2024 election so that the president could remain in office after the end of his constitutionally limited second term. Calling this effort a "constitutional coup," the leader of one of the major confederations proclaimed: "If we're forced, we will oppose this with people power" (Siswanto 2022).

a chance to recover from the brutal crackdown, the government began its campaign of intimidation of independent unions, which tied them up in court and strained organizational resources (Ford et al. 2021). The series of repressive tactics deployed over several years, and that targeted not only labor but also other civil society organizations and opposition parties, disorganized labor internally, and preempted broad-based pushback by forcing each group to fight for its own survival.

The experience of Cambodia and Indonesia illustrates the increasingly sophisticated tactics deployed by authoritarian regimes and autocratizing elites in the region (Curato and Fossati 2020; Morgenbesser 2020). These authoritarian innovations pose a threat not only to opposition parties, the press, human rights groups, and democratic guardrails but also to the region's most dynamic labor movements. Although the situation is dire, this Element should not end on such a bleak note. In 2000, no scholar of Indonesian politics would have anticipated the rising prominence and impact of its labor movement a decade later. Unions there continue to organize, workers still protest and strike, and as this Element goes to press, several Indonesian unions are feverishly preparing for the 2024 elections, which they hope to contest with a revamped Labor Party that is also supported by other popular organizations. In 2010, few would have predicted that Myanmar's young and relatively inexperienced labor movement would be at the forefront of defending democracy in the region in 2021. Backlashes are inevitable, but the struggle continues.

Appendix

The de jure collective rights (DJCR) index evaluates the conformity of national labor legislation with ILO Conventions No. 87 and No. 98 on eighteen indicators pertaining to freedom of association, the right to bargain collectively, and the right to strike. This index is adapted from the index developed by Katrina Burgess and the author for a special issue on labor rights in the journal *Studies in Comparative International Development* published in 2009 (45:2).[1] The formula for calculating the DJCR is unchanged, but I have made some adjustments to the indicators coded, the scoring criteria for some indicators, and the weights given to some indicators.

First, the new index gives greater weight to exclusions from the right to form unions (from 2.0 to 2.5), reduces the weight of exclusions for strikes (from 2.0 to 1.0), and provides more guidance on coding these exclusions.

Second, the indicator for the scope and level of collective bargaining, weighted at 1.5 previously, is now split into two separate indicators, each weighted at 1.0, and the two indicators for ratification of ILO conventions were dropped.[2]

Third, two new indicators were added for the right to strike—definition of a dispute and the legality of replacement workers—weighted at 0.5 each.

Finally, in the original index, countries had to be scored 1 or 0. For several indicators (2, 3, 4, 7, 9, 10, 11, 14, 15), scores of 0.5 are permitted under these circumstances: a) if only a subset of workers (e.g., civil servants) are affected, b) to distinguish between the number of hurdles to striking (i.e., one versus two or more), and c) to distinguish between countries that have no restrictions on the use of replacement workers versus those that only permit them when authorized by the state.

---

[1] See Caraway (2009) for a discussion of the relative merits of this index compared to other indices at the time. Since this index was developed, the most comprehensive system for assessing de jure and de facto labor rights is the Center for Global Workers' Rights Labour Rights Indicators (http://labour-rights-indicators.la.psu.edu/). This comprehensive index has 108 different indicators for de jure and de facto labor rights. The main drawback of this index is that for countries such as Laos and Vietnam where states impose mono-unionism, the index defaults to the worst score, 10. In my view, this coding decision presents a distorted picture of labor rights in Southeast Asia and obfuscates important differences among countries that impose mono-unionism.

  I considered using the weighted (non-normalized) scores in lieu of updating the Burgess and Caraway index, since this avoids the problem outlined above. However, certain anomalies in the scores gave me pause. For example, Malaysia's de jure score is much worse than Singapore's (41.94 versus 29.2), which is too large a difference. Labor rights are worse in Malaysia, but not that much worse. Indonesia, by contrast, which has far less restrictive labor laws, scores about the same as Singapore.

[2] Countries may ratify a convention but still have many legal provisions that violate it. In other words, ratification of a convention has no binding effect on a country to change its laws, so for a de jure measure, it is better to code the actual laws on the books.

The indicators, their weights, and maximum scores are listed in Table A1. See Caraway (2009) for an explanation of how the DJCR is calculated from these scores/weights.

Table A1: De Jure Collective Rights

Freedom of Association		
Indicator	**Weight**	**Maximum scores**
1. General prohibition on unions	15	Subindicators not coded and country receives the max score of 15
2. Administrative or legal hurdles to forming unions	1.5	Max score 1.5
3. Limits on kinds of unions or worker organizations	1.5	Max score 1.5
4. Closed shop or other prohibitions against union pluralism	1.5	Max score 1.5
5. Exclusion from union membership	1.0	Max score 2.5 – scored 1/1/.5 for up to three exclusions (civil servants, teachers, state enterprise workers, Export Processing Zones (EPZ)/other)
6. State interference in internal union affairs	1.5	Max score 1.5
7. General prohibition of union/ federation participation in political activities	1.5	Max score 1.5
Right to Bargain Collectively		
8. General prohibition	10	Subindicators not coded and country receives the max score of 10
9. Restriction on scope of collective bargaining	1.0	Max score 1.0

Table A1: (cont.)

Freedom of Association		
Indicator	**Weight**	**Maximum scores**
10. Restriction on level of collective bargaining	1.0	Max score 1.0
11. Other administrative or legal hurdles	1.0	Max score 1.0
12. Exclusion of unionized sectors from right to bargain	1.0	Max score 2.0 – scored 1/1 for up to two exclusions (civil servants, teachers, state enterprise workers, EPZs/other
Right to strike		
13. General prohibition	10	Subindicators not coded and country receives the max score of 10
14. Binding arbitration	1.5	Max score 1.5
15. Other administrative or legal hurdles	1.5	Max score 1.5
16. Definition of dispute	0.5	Max score 1.0
17. Replacement workers permitted	0.5	Max score 1.0
18. Exclusion of unionized sectors from right to strike	1.0	Max score 2.0 – scored 1/1 for up to two exclusions (civil servants, teachers, state enterprise workers, EPZs/other

References

Aganon, Marie E., Melisa R. Serrano, Rosalinda C. Mercado, and Ramon A. Certeza. 2008. *Revitalizing Philippine Unions: Potentials and Constraints to Social Movement Unionism*. Philippines: Friedrich Ebert Stiftung and U.P. School of Labor and Industrial Relations.

Amante, Maragtas S. V. 2019. "Philippines Unionism–Worker Voice, Representation and Pluralism in Industrial Relations." Interim Report. IDE-JETRO. www.ide.go.jp/library/Japanese/Publish/Reports/Interim Report/2018/pdf/2018_2_40_009_ch04.pdf.

Anderson, Benedict. 1977. "Withdrawal Symptoms: Social and Cultural Aspects of the October 6 Coup." *Bulletin of Concerned Asian Scholars* 9 (3): 13–30. https://doi.org/10.1080/14672715.1977.10406423.

1988. "Cacique Democracy and the Philippines: Origins and Dreams." *New Left Review* I (169): 3–31. https://newleftreview.org/issues/i169/articles/benedict-anderson-cacique-democracy-and-the-philippines-origins-and-dreams

Anner, Mark. 2015. "Labor Control Regimes and Worker Resistance in Global Supply Chains." *Labor History* 56 (3): 292–307. https://doi.org/10.1080/0023656X.2015.1042771.

Anner, Mark, and Xiangmin Liu. 2016. "Harmonious Unions and Rebellious Workers: A Study of Wildcat Strikes in Vietnam." *ILR Review* 69 (1): 3–28. https://doi.org/10.1177/0019793915594596.

Anonymous. 2021. "The Centrality of the Civil Disobedience Movement (CDM) in Myanmar's Post-Coup Era." Policy Briefing – SEARBO. Canberra: Australian National University.

APHEDA. 2018. "Timor Leste: Unions Continue to Fight for Workers' Rights against a Backdrop of Instability." *Union Aid Abroad-APHEDA* (blog). June 28, 2018. www.apheda.org.au/timor-leste-workers-rights/.

Arnold, Dennis. 2013. "Workers' Agency and Re-Working Power Relations in Cambodia's Garment Industry." Working Paper No. 24. Capturing the Gains. Manchester: University of Manchester.

2017. "Civil Society, Political Society and Politics of Disorder in Cambodia." *Political Geography* 60 (September): 23–33. https://doi.org/10.1016/j.polgeo.2017.03.008.

Arnold, Dennis, and Stephen Campbell. 2017. "Labour Regime Transformation in Myanmar: Constitutive Processes of Contestation." *Development and Change* 48 (4): 801–24. https://doi.org/10.1111/dech.12315.

Arnold, Dennis, and Toh Han Shih. 2010. "A Fair Model of Globalisation? Labour and Global Production in Cambodia." *Journal of Contemporary Asia* 40 (3): 401–24. https://doi.org/10.1080/00472331003798376.

Arudsothy, Ponniah, and Craig R. Littler. 1993. "State Regulation and Union Fragmentation in Malaysia." In *Organized Labor in the Asia-Pacific Region: A Comparative Study of Trade Unionism in Nine Countries*, edited by Stephen Frenkel, 107–30. Ithaca: Cornell University/ILR Press.

Asia Monitor Resource Centre, Asian Labour Study Group, Asian Human Rights Commission, Korean Confederation of Trade Unions, Oxfam Solidarity Belgium, Center for Trade Unions and Human Rights, Korean House for International Solidarity, and Serve People Association. 2014. "A Week That Shook Cambodia." Hong Kong: AMRC.

Aspinall, Edward. 1999. "Democratisation, the Working Class and the Indonesian Transition." *Review of Indonesian and Malayan Affairs* 33: 1–31.

Aspinall, Edward, and Marcus Mietzner. 2019. "Indonesia's Democratic Paradox: Competitive Elections amidst Rising Illiberalism." *Bulletin of Indonesian Economic Studies* 55 (3): 295–317.

Asuyama, Yoko, and Seiha Neou. 2014. "Cambodia: Growth with Better Working Conditions." In *The Garment Industry in Low-Income Countries: An Entry Point of Industrialization*, edited by Takahiro Fukunishi and Tatsufumi Yamagata, 38–76. New York: Palgrave Macmillan.

Ativanichayapong, Napaporn. 2002. "Social Movement Unionism and Economic Unionism in Thailand." *Asian Review*, 15: 78–103.

Barr, Michael D. 2000. "Trade Unions in an Elitist Society: The Singapore Story." *Australian Journal of Politics and History* 46: 480–96.

Bellin, Eva. 2002. *Stalled Democracy: Capital, Labor, and the Paradox of State-Sponsored Development*. Ithaca: Cornell University Press.

Beng, Chew Soon, and Ryan Tan Hin Tuan. 2020. "From Worker Representation to Worker Empowerment: The Case of Singapore." In *Trade Unions and Labour Movements in the Asia-Pacific Region*, edited by Byoung-Hoon Lee, Sek-Hong Ng, and Russell D. Lansbury, 204–21. New York: Routledge.

Beresford, Melanie. 2006. "Vietnam: The Transition from Central Planning." In *The Political Economy of South-East Asia: Markets, Power and Contestation*, edited by Garry Rodan, Kevin Hewison, and Richard Robison, 197–220. New York: Oxford University Press.

Beresford, Melanie, and Chris Nyland. 1998. "The Labour Movement of Vietnam." *Labour History* 75 (Novemberr): 57–80. https://doi.org/10.2307/27516602.

Better Factories Cambodia. 2009. "Twenty-Third Synthesis Report on Working Conditions in Cambodia's Garment Sector." Geneva: International Labour Office.

2018. "Annual Report 2018: An Industry and Compliance Review." Geneva: International Labour Office.

Bhopal, Mhinder. 2001. "Malaysian Unions in Political Crisis: Assessing the Impact of the Asian Contagion." *Asia Pacific Business Review* 8 (2): 73–100. https://doi.org/10.1080/713999143.

Boudreau, Vincent. 2004. *Resisting Dictatorship: Repression and Protest in Southeast Asia*. New York: Cambridge University Press.

Bronstein, Arturo. 2005. "The Role of the International Labour Office in the Framing of National Labor Law." *Comparative Labor Law & Policy Journal* 26: 339–69.

Brown, Andrew. 2003. *Labor, Politics and the State in Industrializing Thailand*. New York: RoutledgeCurzon.

Brown, Andrew, and Chatrakul Na Ayudhya Sakdina. 2013. "Labour Activism in Thailand." In *Social Activism in Asia*, edited by Michele Ford, 104–18. New York: Routledge.

Brown, Andrew, and Kevin Hewison. 2004. "Labor Politics in Thaksin's Thailand." Working Paper No. 62. Hong Kong: City University of Hong Kong Southeast Asia Research Center.

Buckley, Joe. 2020. "The Role of Labour Activism in Vietnam's Coronavirus Success." *Equal Times* (blog). 2 July 2020. www.equaltimes.org/the-role-of-labour-activism-in?lang=en#.YNR-AxNKhmB.

2021a. "Freedom of Association in Vietnam: A Heretical View." *Global Labour Journal* 12 (2): 79–94. https://doi.org/10.15173/glj.v12i2.4442.

2021b. *Vietnamese Labour Militancy: Capital-Labour Antagonisms and Self-Organised Struggles*. New York: Routledge.

Bünte, Marco. 2022. "Ruling but Not Governing: Tutelary Regimes and the Case of Myanmar." *Government and Opposition* 57 (2): 336–52. https://doi.org/10.1017/gov.2020.38.

Burgess, Katrina. 2004. *Parties and Unions in the New Global Economy*. Pittsburgh: University of Pittsburgh Press.

2010. "Global Pressures, National Policies, and Labor Rights in Latin America." *Studies in Comparative International Development* 45 (2): 198–224.

Bynum, Elliott, and Franziska Pfadt. 2019. "Increased Repression, Declining Demonstrations: An Analysis of Cambodian Demonstrations (2010–2018)." *ACLED* (blog). 22 February 2019. https://acleddata.com/2019/02/22/increased-repression-declining-demonstrations-an-analysis-of-cambodian-demonstrations-2010-2018/.

Caraway, Teri L. 2004. "Protective Repression, International Pressure, and Institutional Design: Explaining Labor Reform in Indonesia." *Studies in Comparative International Development* 39 (3): 28–49.

2006. "Freedom of Association: Battering Ram or Trojan Horse?" *Review of International Political Economy* 13 (2): 210–32.

2007. *Assembling Women: The Feminization of Global Manufacturing.* Ithaca: ILR Press.

2009. "Labor Rights in Asia: Progress or Regress?" *Journal of East Asian Studies* 9 (2): 153–86.

2010. "Core Labor Rights in Indonesia 2010: A Survey of Violations in the Formal Sector." Jakarta: American Center for International Labor Solidarity.

2013. "Labor Courts in Indonesia." Jakarta: American Center for International Labor Solidarity.

Forthcoming a. "Labor's Reversal of Fortune: Contentious Politics and Executive Aggrandizement in Indonesia." *Social Movement Studies.* www.tandfonline.com/doi/abs/10.1080/14742837.2021.2010529.

Forthcoming b. "Organized Labor and Autocratization in Southeast Asia." In *Routledge Handbook of Civil Society and Uncivil Society in Southeast Asia*, edited by Eva Hansson and Meredith Weiss. New York: Routledge.

Caraway, Teri L., Maria Lorena Cook, and Stephen Crowley, eds. 2015. *Working Through the Past: Labor and Authoritarian Legacies in Comparative Perspective.* Ithaca: ILR Press.

Caraway, Teri L., and Michele Ford. 2014. "Labor Politics Under Oligarchy." In *Beyond Oligarchy? Critical Exchanges on Political Power and Material Inequality in Indonesia*, edited by Michele Ford and Thomas Pepinsky, 139–56. Ithaca: Cornell Southeast Asia Program.

2020. *Labor and Politics in Indonesia.* New York: Cambridge University Press.

Caraway, Teri L., Michele Ford, and Oanh K. Nguyen. 2019. "Politicizing the Minimum Wage: Wage Councils, Worker Mobilization, and Local Elections in Indonesia." *Politics & Society* 47 (2): 251–76.

Caraway, Teri L., Michele Ford, and Hari Nugroho. 2015. "Translating Membership into Power at the Ballot Box? Trade Union Candidates and Worker Voting Patterns in Indonesia's National Elections." *Democratization* 22 (7): 1296–316.

Carew, Anthony. 1996. "Conflict Within the ICFTU: Anti-Communism and Anti-Colonialism in the 1950s." *International Review of Social History* 41 (2): 147–81. https://doi.org/10.1017/S0020859000113859.

Chan, Chris King-Chi, and Elaine Sio-Ieng Hui. 2022. "Pension Systems and Labour Resistance in Post-Socialist China and Vietnam: A Welfare

Regime Analysis." *Journal of Contemporary Asia* 0 (0): 1–20. https://doi .org/10.1080/00472336.2021.2016246.

Chin, James. 2022. "Malaysia in 2021: Another Regime Change and the Search for Malay Political Stability." *Southeast Asian Affairs* 2022 (1): 195–210.

Clarke, Simon. 2006. "The Changing Character of Strikes in Vietnam." *Post-Communist Economies* 18 (3): 345–61. https://doi.org/10.1080/14631 370600881796.

Clarke, Simon, Chang-Hee Lee, and Do Quynh Chi. 2007. "From Rights to Interests: The Challenge of Industrial Relations in Vietnam:" *Journal of Industrial Relations* 49 (4): 545–68. https://doi.org/10.1177/002218 5607080321.

Collins, Ngan. 2020. "The Reform of Vietnam Trade Union and the Government's Role Since Doi Moi." In *Trade Unions and Labour Movements in the Asia-Pacific Region*, edited by Byoung-Hoon Lee, Sek-Hong Ng, and Russell D. Lansbury, 273–92. New York: Routledge.

Connell, Tula. 2021. "Two Women Union Leaders Arrested in Myanmar; Total Now 20+." *Solidarity Center* (blog). April 29, 2021. www.solidaritycenter .org/two-women-union-leaders-arrested-in-myanmar-total-now-20/.

Cook, Linda. 2010. "More Rights, Less Power: Labor Standards and Labor Markets in East European Post-Communist States." *Studies in Comparative International Development* 45 (2): 170–97.

Cook, Maria Lorena. 2007. *The Politics of Labor Reform in Latin America: Between Flexibility and Rights*. University Park: Pennsylvania State University Press.

Crowley, Stephen. 2004. "Explaining Labor Weakness in Post-Communist Europe: Historical Legacies and Comparative Perspective." *East European Politics and Societies* 18: 394–429.

Crowley, Stephen, and David Ost. 2001. *Workers after Workers' States: Labor and Politics in Postcommunist Eastern Europe*. New York: Rowman & Littlefield.

Curato, Nicole, and Diego Fossati. 2020. "Authoritarian Innovations: Crafting Support for a Less Democratic Southeast Asia." *Democratization* 27 (6): 1006–20.

Davidson, Jamie S. 2018. *Indonesia: Twenty Years of Democracy*. New York: Cambridge University Press. www.cambridge.org/core/elements/indonesia/ 8E0D464AFC077007052B28FF16F7C287.

Dejillas, Leopoldo J. 1994. *Trade Union Behavior in the Philippines, 1946–1990*. Manila: Ateneo de Manila University Press.

Devinatz, Victor G. 2013. "A Cold War Thaw in the International Working Class Movement? The World Federation of Trade Unions and the International Confederation of Free Trade Unions, 1967–1977." *Science & Society* 77 (3): 342–71. https://doi.org/10.1521/siso.2013.77.3.342.

Deyo, Frederic C. 1981. *Dependent Development and Industrial Order.* New York: Praeger.

———. 1989. *Beneath the Miracle: Labor Subordination in the New Asian Industrialism.* Berkeley: University of California.

———. 1997. "Labour and Industrial Restructuring in South-East Asia." In *The Political Economy of South-East Asia: An Introduction*, edited by Garry Rodan, Kevin Hewison, and Richard Robison, 205–24. New York: Oxford University Press.

———. 2001. "The Social Construction of Developmental Labour Systems: South-East Asian Industrial Restructuring." In *The Political Economy of South-East Asia: Conflicts, Crises, and Change*, edited by Garry Rodan, Kevin Hewison, and Richard Robison, 259–82. New York: Oxford University Press.

———. 2012. *Reforming Asian Labor Systems: Economic Tensions and Worker Dissent.* Ithaca: Cornell University Press.

Do, Quynh Chi. 2017. "The Regional Coordination of Strikes and the Challenge for Union Reform in Vietnam." *Development and Change* 48 (5): 1052–68. https://doi.org/10.1111/dech.12326.

Doutch, Michaela. 2021. "A Gendered Labour Geography Perspective on the Cambodian Garment Workers' General Strike of 2013/2014." *Globalizations* 18 (8): 1406–19. https://doi.org/10.1080/14747731.2021.1877007.

Dunkley, Graham. 1982. "Industrial Relations and Labour in Malaysia." *Journal of Industrial Relations* 24 (3): 424–42. https://doi.org/10.1177/002218568202400306.

Edwards, Vincent, and Anh Phan. 2008. "Trade Unions in Vietnam: From Socialism to Market Socialism." In *Trade Unions in Asia: An Economic and Sociological Analysis*, edited by John Benson and Ying Zhu, 199–215. New York: Routledge.

Evans, Allison D., and Rudra Sil. 2020. "The Dynamics of Labor Militancy in the Extractive Sector: Kazakhstan's Oilfields and South Africa's Platinum Mines in Comparative Perspective." *Comparative Political Studies* 53 (6): 992–1024. https://doi.org/10.1177/0010414019879715.

Fong, Pang Eng, and Chwee Huat Tan. 1983. "Trade Unions and Industrial Relations." In *Singapore: Development Policies and Trends*, edited by Peter S. J. Chen, 227–39. New York: Oxford University Press.

Ford, Michele. 1999. "Testing the Limits of Corporatism: Reflections on Industrial Relations Institutions and Practice in Suharto's Indonesia." *Journal of Industrial Relations* 41: 371–92.

2000. "Continuity and Change in Indonesian Labour Relations in the Habibie Interregnum." *Southeast Asian Journal of Social Science* 28: 59–88.

2009. *Workers and Intellectuals: NGOs, Trade Unions and the Indonesian Labour Movement*. Singapore: NUS/Hawaii/KITLV.

2016. "The Making of Industrial Relations in Timor-Leste." *Journal of Industrial Relations* 58 (2): 243–57.

Ford, Michele, and Kristy Ward. 2021. "COVID-19 in Southeast Asia: Implications for Workers and Unions." *Journal of Industrial Relations* 63 (3): 432–50. https://doi.org/10.1177/00221856211000097.

Ford, Michele, Michael Gillan, and Kristy Ward. 2021. "Authoritarian Innovations in Labor Governance: The Case of Cambodia." *Governance* 34(3): 1255–71. https://doi.org/10.1111/gove.12559.

Franceschini, Ivan. 2020. "At the Roots of Labour Activism: Chinese and Cambodian Garment Workers in Comparative Perspective." *Journal of Contemporary Asia* 50 (1): 144–67. https://doi.org/10.1080/00472336 .2018.1555272.

Fry, Simon. 2008. "Three Transformations of Industrial Relations in Laos." *Journal of Industrial Relations* 50 (5): 779–95. https://doi.org/10.1177/ 0022185608094117.

Fry, Simon. 2012. "The Lao Federation of Trade Unions: A Classic Dualist Union," *International Journal of Employment Studies* 20(2): 32–54.

Fry, Simon, and Bernard Mees. 2016. "Industrial Relations in Asian Socialist-Transition Economies: China, Vietnam and Laos." *Post-Communist Economies* 28 (4): 449–67. https://doi.org/10.1080/14631377 .2016.1225450.

Gerschenkron, Alexander. 1962. *Economic Backwardness in Historical Perspective*. Cambridge, MA: Harvard University Press.

Gillan, Michael, and Htwe Htwe Thein. 2016. "Employment Relations, the State and Transitions in Governance in Myanmar." *Journal of Industrial Relations* 58 (2): 273–88. https://doi.org/10.1177/0022185615617570.

Glasius, Marlies. 1999. *Foreign Policy on Human Rights: Its Influence on Indonesia under Suharto*. Antwerpen: Intersentia-Hart.

Glassman, Jim. 2004. *Thailand at the Margins: Internationalization of the State and the Transformation of Labour*. New York: Oxford University Press.

Global Labor Justice-International Labor Rights Forum. 2021. "Request for Review of the GSP Status of the Republic of the Philippines for Violations of Worker Rights." https://laborrights.org/publications/request-review-gsp-status-republic-philippines-violations-worker-rights.

Haack, Michael, and Nadi Hlaing. 2021. "Workers in Myanmar Are Launching General Strikes to Resist the Coup: An Interview with Ma Moe Sandar Mying, Ma Ei Ei Phyu, Ma Tin Tin Wai." *Jacobin* (blog). March 9, 2021. https://jacobinmag.com/2021/03/myanmar-burma-general-strike-coup.

Hadiz, Vedi. 1997. *Workers and the State in New Order Indonesia*. New York: Routledge.

Haggard, Stephan. 1990. *Pathways from the Periphery: The Politics of Growth in the Newly Industrializing Countries*. Ithaca: Cornell University Press.

Hall, John A. 2000. "Human Rights and the Garment Industry in Contemporary Cambodia Note." *Stanford Journal of International Law* 36 (1): 119–74.

—— 2010. "The ILO's Better Factories Cambodia Program: A Viable Blueprint for Promoting International Labor Rights?" *Stanford Law & Policy Review* 21 (3): 427.

Han, Kirsten. 2018. "Recalling Singapore's Forgotten Unions." *People's World* (blog). February 12, 2018. www.peoplesworld.org/article/recalling-singapores-forgotten-unions/.

Hansson, Eva. 2003. "Authoritarian Governance and Labour: The VGCL and the Party-State in Economic Renovation." In *Getting Organized in Vietnam: Moving In and around the Socialist State*, edited by Benedict J. Tria Kerkvliet, Russell H. K. Heng, and David W. H. Kho, 153–84. Singapore: Institute of Southeast Asian Studies.

Hansson, Eva, Kevin Hewison, and Jim Glassman. 2020. "Legacies of the Cold War in East and Southeast Asia: An Introduction." *Journal of Contemporary Asia* 50 (4): 493–510. https://doi.org/10.1080/00472336.2020.1758955.

Hawkins, E. D. 1971. "Labor in Developing Countries: Indonesia." In *The Indonesian Economy: Selected Readings*, edited by Bruce Glassburner, 196–250. Ithaca: Cornell University.

Henry, Nicholas. 2015. "Trade Union Internationalism and Political Change in Myanmar." *Global Change, Peace & Security* 27 (1): 69–84. https://doi.org/10.1080/14781158.2015.997688.

—— 2016. "Everyday Agents of Change: Trade Unions in Myanmar." In *The Everyday Political Economy of Southeast Asia*, edited by Juanita Elias and Lena Rethel, 72–92. New York: Cambridge University Press.

Hewison, Kevin. 1997. "Thailand: Capitalist Development and the State." In *The Political Economy of South-East Asia: An Introduction*, edited by Garry Rodan, Kevin Hewison, and Richard Robison, 93–120. New York: Oxford University Press.

2020. "Black Site: The Cold War and the Shaping of Thailand's Politics." *Journal of Contemporary Asia* 50 (4): 551–70. https://doi.org/10.1080/00472336.2020.1717115.

Hewison, Kevin, and Garry Rodan. 1994. "The Decline of the Left in Southeast Asia." *Socialist Register* 30: 235–62.

Hewison, Kevin, and Woradul Tularak. 2013. "Thailand and Precarious Work: An Assessment." *American Behavioral Scientist* 57 (4): 444–67. https://doi.org/10.1177/0002764212466244.

Hughes, Caroline. 2007. "Transnational Networks, International Organizations and Political Participation in Cambodia: Human Rights, Labour Rights and Common Rights." *Democratization* 14 (5): 834–52. https://doi.org/10.1080/13510340701635688.

Human Rights Watch. 2015. "'Work Faster or Get Out': Labor Rights Abuses in Cambodia's Garment Industry." New York: Human Rights Watch.

Hutchison, Jane. 1997. "Pressure on Policy in the Philippines." In *The Political Economy of Southeast Asia: An Introduction*, edited by Garry Rodan, Kevin Hewison, and Richard Robison, 64–92. New York: Oxford University Press.

2015. "Authoritarian Labor Legacies in the Philippines." In *Working Through the Past: Labor and Authoritarian Legacies in Comparative Perspective*, edited by Teri L. Caraway, Maria Lorena Cook, and Stephen Crowley, 64–81. Ithaca: ILR Press.

Hutchison, Jane, and Andrew Brown. 2001. *Organizing Labor in Globalizing Asia*. New York: Routledge.

Indonesian Documentation and Information Centre. 1981. *Indonesian Workers and Their Right to Organise*. Leiden: INDOC.

INDUSTRIALL. 2020. "Global Unions Condemn Philippines Anti-Terrorism Act." July 15, 2020. www.industriall-union.org/global-unions-condemn-philippines-anti-terrorism-act.

International Labour Office. 1997. *World Labour Report: Industrial Relations, Democracy and Social Stability*. Geneva: ILO.

2001. "Substantive Provisions of Labour Legislation: The Right to Strike." In *Labour Legislation Guideline*. https://www.ilo.org/legacy/english/dialogue/ifpdial/llg/index.htm. www.ilo.org/legacy/english/dialogue/ifpdial/llg/noframes/ch5.htm.

2017a. "Observation (CEACR), Freedom of Association and Protection of the Right to Organise Convention, 1948 (No. 87)." ILO Geneva.

2017b. "Observation (CEACR), Right to Organise and Collective Bargaining Convention, 1949 (No. 98)." ILO Geneva.

Jomo, K. S., and Patricia Todd. 1994. *Trade Unions and the State in Peninsular Malaysia*. New York: Oxford University Press.

Jordt, Ingrid, Tharaphi Than, and Sue Ye Lin. 2021. *How Generation Z Galvanized a Revolutionary Movement against Myanmar's 2021 Military Coup*. Singapore: ISEAS–Yusof Ishak Institute. https://book shop.iseas.edu.sg/publication/2494.

Juliawan, Benny Hari. 2010. "Extracting Labor From Its Owner." *Critical Asian Studies* 42: 25–52.

Kahin, Audrey R., and George McT. Kahin. 1995. *Subversion as Foreign Policy: The Secret Eisenhower and Dulles Debacle in Indonesia*. Seattle: University of Washington Press.

Kammen, Douglas. 1997. "A Time to Strike: Industrial Strikes and Changing Class Relations in New Order Indonesia." Unpublished PhD dissertation. Ithaca: Cornell University.

Kasian, Tejapira. 2006. "Toppling Thaksin." *New Left Review* 39 (May-June): 5–37.

Kerkvliet, Benedict J. 1977. *The Huk Rebellion: A Study of Peasant Revolt in the Philippines*. Berkeley: University of California Press.

Kerkvliet, Benedict J. Tria. 2010. "Workers' Protests in Contemporary Vietnam (with Some Comparisons to Those in the Pre-1975 South)." *Journal of Vietnamese Studies* 5 (1): 162–204. https://doi.org/10.1525/vs.2010.5.1.162.

Kiernan, Ben. 2002. "Introduction: Conflict in Cambodia, 1945–2002." *Critical Asian Studies* 34 (4): 483–95.

Kuruvilla, Sarosh. 1996. "Linkages between Industrialization Strategies and Industrial Relations/Human Resource Policies: Singapore, Malaysia, the Philippines, and India." *Industrial & Labor Relations Review* 49: 635–57.

Kyaw, Soe Lwin. 2013. "The Evolution of Labour Politics in Post-Colonial Myanmar." Unpublished PhD dissertation. Kowloon Tong: City Universtiy of Hong Kong.

Labour Behind the Label, and Cambodian Legal Education Centre. 2013. "Shop 'til They Drop: Fainting and Malnutrition in Garment Workers in Cambodia." LBL and CLEC. https://cleanclothes.org/resources/national-cccs/shop-til-they-drop.

Landau, Ingrid. 2008. "Law and Civil Society in Cambodia and Vietnam: A Gramscian Perspective." *Journal of Contemporary Asia* 38 (2): 244–58. https://doi.org/10.1080/00472330701822322.

Landau, Ingrid, Petra Mahy, and Richard Mitchell. 2015. "The Regulation of Non-Standard Forms of Employment in India, Indonesia and Viet Nam." Geneva: International Labor Office.

Lawreniuk, Sabina. 2020. "Intensifying Political Geographies of Authoritarianism: Toward an Anti-Geopolitics of Garment Worker Struggles in Neoliberal Cambodia." *Annals of the American Association of Geographers* 110 (4): 1174–91. https://doi.org/10.1080/24694452.2019.1670040.

———. Forthcoming. "Zombie Resistance: Reanimated Labour Struggles and the Legal Geographies of Authoritarian Neoliberalism in Cambodia." *Transactions of the Institute of British Geographers*. https://doi.org/10.1111/tran.12564.

Lee, Chang-Hee. 2006. "Industrial Relations and Dispute Settlement in Vietnam." Discussion Paper. Hanoi: International Labor Office.

Leggett, Chris. 1984. "Airline Pilots and Public Industrial Relations: The Case of Singapore Airlines." *Indian Journal of Industrial Relations* 20 (1): 27–43.

———. 1988. "Industrial Relations and Enterprise Unionism in Singapore." *Labor & Industry* 1: 242–57.

———. 1993. "Singapore." In *Labor Law and Industrial Relations in Asia: Eight Country Studies*, edited by Stephen Deery and Richard Mitchell, 96–136. Melbourne: Longman Cheshire.

———. 2008. "Trade Unions in Singapore: Corporatist Paternalism." In *Trade Unions in Asia: An Economic and Sociological Analysis*, edited by John Benson and Ying Zhu, 102–20. New York: Routledge.

Lev, Daniel S. 2009. *The Transition to Guided Democracy: Indonesian Politics, 1957–1959*. Jakarta: Equinox.

Levenson, Zachary. 2021. "Keep the Streets: Coup, Crisis, and Capital in Myanmar: Interview with Geoffrey Aung." *Spectrejournal.Com* (blog). February 20, 2021. https://spectrejournal.com/keep-the-streets-coup-crisis-and-capitalism-in-myanmar/.

Lowenstein, Allard K. 2011. "Tearing Apart at the Seams: How Widespread Use of Fixed-Duration Contracts Threatens Cambodian Workers and the Cambodian Garment Industry." International Human Rights Clinic. New Haven: Yale Law School.

Luther, Hans U. 1978. "Strikes and the Institutionalization of Labor Protest: The Case of Singapore." *Journal of Contemporary Asia* 8: 219–30.

Mabry, Bevars D., and Kundhol Srisermbhok. 1985. "Labor Relations under Martial Law: The Thailand Experience." *Asian Survey* 25 (June): 613–37.

Magadia, Jose J. 2003. *State-Society Dynamics: Policy Making in a Restored Democracy*. Manila: Ateneo University Press.

Manning, Christopher Gibson. 1998. *Indonesian Labour in Transition: An East Asian Success Story?* New York: Cambridge University Press.

McCargo, Duncan. 2005. "Network Monarchy and Legitimacy Crises in Thailand." *The Pacific Review* 18 (4): 499–519. https://doi.org/10.1080/09512740500338937.

2021. "Disruptors' Dilemma? Thailand's 2020 Gen Z Protests." *Critical Asian Studies* 53 (2): 175–91. https://doi.org/10.1080/14672715.2021.1876522.

Mietzner, Marcus. 2012. "Indonesia's Democratic Stagnation: Anti-Reformist Elites and Resilient Civil Society." *Democratization* 19: 209–29.

2021. "Sources of Resistance to Democratic Decline: Indonesian Civil Society and Its Trials." *Democratization* 28 (1): 161–78.

Morell, David, and Samutwanit Chai'anan. 1981. *Political Conflict in Thailand: Reform, Reaction, Revolution.* Cambridge: Oelgeschlager, Gunn & Hain.

Morgan, Michael. 1977. "The Rise and Fall of Malayan Trade Unionism, 1945–50." In *Malaya: The Making of a Neo-Colony*, edited by Mohammed Amin and Malcolm Caldwell, 150–98. Nottingham: Spokesman.

Morgenbesser, Lee. 2020. *The Rise of Sophisticated Authoritarianism in Southeast Asia.* New York: Cambridge University Press.

Mortimer, Rex. 2006. *Indonesian Communism Under Sukarno: Ideology and Politics, 1959–1965.* Singapore: Equinox.

Mufakhir, Abu. 2014. "'Grebek Pabrik' in Bekasi: Research Note on Unions' Mobilisation Strategy." In *Worker Activism after Reformasi 1998: A New Phase for Indonesian Unions?*, edited by Jafar Suryomenggolo, 93–114. Hong Kong: Asia Monitor Resource Centre.

Mufakhir, Abu, and Alifan Alayubi Pelu. 2015. "Ketika Kepolisian Melanggar Undang-Undang: Kasus Represi Terhadap Demonstrasi Damai Buruh." *IndoPROGRESS* (blog). November 11, 2015. https://indoprogress.com/2015/11/ketika-kepolisian-melanggar-undang-undang-kasus-represi-terhadap-demonstrasi-damai-buruh/.

New Straits Times. 2020. "Thousands Protest in Yangon for Higher Minimum Wage." *NST Online*, January 21, 2020, sec. region. www.nst.com.my/world/region/2020/01/558348/thousands-protest-yangon-higher-minimum-wage.

Nørlund, Irene. 2004. "Trade Unions in Vietnam in Historical Perspective: The Transformation of Concepts." In *Labor in Southeast Asia: Local Processes in a Globalised World*, edited by Rebecca Elmhirst and Ratna Saptari, 108–28. New York: Routledge.

Nuon, Veasna, and Melisa Serrano. 2010. *Building Unions in Cambodia: History, Challenges, Strategies.* Singapore: Friedrich Ebert Stiftung.

O'Donnell, Guillermo A. 1973. *Modernization and Bureaucratic-Authoritarianism: Studies in South American Politics*. Berkeley: University of California Institute of International Studies.

Ofreneo, Rene E. 2013. "Precarious Philippines: Expanding Informal Sector, 'Flexibilizing' Labor Market." *American Behavioral Scientist* 57 (4): 420–43. https://doi.org/10.1177/0002764212466237.

———. 2020. "Worker Representation in a Segmented and Globalised Philippine Economy." In *Trade Unions and Labour Movements in the Asia-Pacific Region*, edited by Byoung-Hoon Lee, Sek-Hong Ng, and Russell D. Lansbury, 185–203. New York: Routledge.

Oka, Chikako. 2016. "Improving Working Conditions in Garment Supply Chains: The Role of Unions in Cambodia." *British Journal of Industrial Relations* 54 (3): 647–72. https://doi.org/10.1111/bjir.12118.

Orejas, Tonette. 2016. "No Justice yet in Luisita Massacre." INQUIRER.Net. November 17, 2016. https://newsinfo.inquirer.net/844943/no-justice-yet-in-luisita-massacre.

Ost, David. 2005. *The Defeat of Solidarity: Anger and Politics in Postcommunist Europe*. Ithaca: Cornell University Press.

Panimbang, Fahmi, and Abu Mufakhir. 2018. "Labour Strikes in Post-Authoritarian Indonesia, 1998–2013." In *Workers' Movements and Strikes in the Twenty-First Century*, edited by Jörg Nowak, Madhumita Dutta, and Peter Birke, 21–41. New York: Rowman & Littlefield.

Piriyarangsan, Sungsidh, and Kanchada Poonpanich. 1994. "Labour Institutions in an Export-Oriented Country: A Case Study of Thailand." In *Workers, Institutions and Economic Growth in Asia*, edited by Gerry Rodgers, 211–53. Geneva: International Institute for Labour Studies.

Polaski, Sandra. 2006. "Combining Global and Local Forces: The Case of Labor Rights in Cambodia." *World Development* 34 (5): 919–32. https://doi.org/10.1016/j.worlddev.2005.04.019.

Pringle, Tim, and Simon Clarke. 2010. *The Challenge of Transition: Trade Unions in Russia, China and Vietnam* (version 2011 ed.). 2011 ed. New York: Palgrave Macmillan.

Quimpo, Nathan Gilbert. 2008. *Contested Democracy and the Left in the Philippines After Marcos*. New Haven: Yale University Southeast Asia Studies.

———. 2014. "Can the Philippines' Wild Oligarchy Be Tamed?" In *Routledge Handbook of Southeast Asian Democratization*, edited by William Case, 347–62. New York: Routledge.

Rajah, Meera. 2019. "'From Third World to First': A Case Study of Labor Laws in a Changing Singapore." *Labor Law Journal* 2019 (Spring): 42–63.

Ramos, Elias T. 1976. *Philippine Labor Movement in Transition*. Quezon City: New Day.

Rasiah, Rajah. 1997. "Class, Ethnicity and Economic Development in Malaysia." In *The Political Economy of South-East Asia: An Introduction*, edited by Garry Rodan, Kevin Hewison, and Richard Robison, 121–47. New York: Oxford University Press.

Ratcliffe, Rebecca. 2021. "Top Thai Union Leader 'Targeted' with Jail for Rail Safety Campaign." *The Guardian*, September 21, 2021. https://www.the guardian.com/global-development/2021/sep/21/top-thai-union-leader-targeted-with-jail-for-rail-safety-campaign.

Reuters. 2009. "ILO Asks Philippines to Probe Trade Union Killings." *Reuters*, October 1, 2009, sec. Latest Crisis. www.reuters.com/article/idUSMAN 159098.

Rhoden, T. F. 2015. "Oligarchy in Thailand?" *Journal of Current Southeast Asian Affairs* 34 (1): 3–25. https://doi.org/10.1177/186810341503400101.

Robertson, Philip S. Jr. 2001. "Driving Forward with Determination: Thai Labor and the Constitution of 1997." In *Thailand's New Politics: King Prajadhipok's Institute Yearbook 2001*, edited by Michael H. Nelson, 95–144. Bangkok: White Lotus Press.

Robinson, Geoffrey B. 2020. *The Killing Season: A History of the Indonesian Massacres, 1965–66*. Princeton: Princeton University Press.

Rodan, Garry. 1997. "Singapore: Economic Diversification and Social Divisions." In *The Political Economy of South-East Asia: An Introduction*, edited by Garry Rodan, Kevin Hewison, and Richard Robison, 148–78. New York: Oxford University Press.

Rodan, Garry, Kevin Hewison, and Richard Robison. 2001. *The Political Economy of South-East Asia: Conflict, Crises, and Change*. New York: Oxford University Press.

Roosa, John. 2006. *Pretext for Mass Murder: The September 30th Movement and Suharto's Coup d'Etat in Indonesia*. Madison: University of Wisconsin Press.

Rowley, Chris, and Mhinder Bhopal. 2006. "The Ethnic Factor in State-Labour Relations: The Case of Malaysia." *Capital & Class* 30 (1): 87–115. https://doi.org/10.1177/030981680608800105.

Rudner, Martin. 1973. "Malayan Labor in Transition Labor Policy and Trade Unionism, 1955–63." *Modern Asian Studies* 7: 21–45.

Rueschemeyer, Dietrich, Evelyne Huber Stephens, and John. D. Stephens. 1992. *Capitalist Development & Democracy*. Chicago: University of Chicago.

Ruji, Auethavornpipat, and Teerakowitkajorn Kriangsak. 2021. "Thai Workers against Dictatorship?" *New Mandala* (blog). June 29, 2021. www.new mandala.org/thai-workers-against-dictatorship/.

Salmivaara, Anna. 2018. "New Governance of Labour Rights: The Perspective of Cambodian Garment Workers' Struggles." *Globalizations* 15 (3): 329–46. https://doi.org/10.1080/14747731.2017.1394069.

Schrank, Delphine. 2021. "Myanmar's Other Government." *The New York Review of Books* (blog). June 7, 2021. www-nybooks-com.ezp1.lib .umn.edu/daily/2021/06/07/myanmars-other-government/.

Schweisshelm, Erwin, and Do Quynh Chi. 2018. "From Harmony to Conflict – Vietnamese Trade Unions on the Threshold of Reform." In *Trade Unions in Transition From Command to Market Economies*, edited by Rudolf Traub-Merz and Tim Pringle, 109–48. Berlin: Friedrich Ebert-Stiftung.

Serrano, Melisa R., ed. 2014. *The Rise of Non-Standard Employment in Selected ASEAN Countries*. Jakarta: ASEAN Services Employees Trade Unions Council.

Sidel, John T. 1998. "The Underside of Progress: Land, Labor, and Violence in Two Philippine Growth Zones, 1985–1995." *Bulletin of Concerned Asian Scholars* 30: 3–12.

Silver, Beverly J. 2003. *Forces of Labor: Workers' Movements and Globalization since 1870*. New York: Cambridge University Press.

Silverstein, Josef. 1977. *Burma: Military Rule and the Politics of Stagnation*. Ithaca: Cornell University Press.

Simpson, Bradley R. 2008. *Economists with Guns: Authoritarian Development and U.S.-Indonesian Relations, 1960–1968*. Stanford: Stanford University Press.

Siswanto. 2022. "Penundaan Pemilu 2024, Said Iqbal: Kami Akan Lawan Dengan People Power Kalau Dipaksakan." *Suara.Com*, March 2, 2022. www.suara.com/news/2022/03/02/145338/penundaan-pemilu-2024-saiq-iqbal-kami-akan-lawan-dengan-people-power-kalau-dipaksakan.

Siu, Kaxton, and Anita Chan. 2015. "Strike Wave in Vietnam, 2006–2011." *Journal of Contemporary Asia* 45 (1): 71–91. https://doi.org/10.1080/00472336.2014.903290.

Siwa, Jane Alexandra, and Jessica Viliran. 2016. "Taming Class Conflict? Industrial Peace and Workers' Resistance in the Philippines, 2001–2016." *Philippine Sociological Review* 64: 41–72.

Snyder, Kay A., and Thomas C. Nowak. 1982. "Philippine Labor Before Martial Law: Threat or Nonthreat?" *Studies in Comparative International Development* 17: 44–72.

Stenson, Michael R. 1970. *Industrial Conflict in Malaya: Prelude to the Communist Revolt of 1948*. New York: Oxford University Press.

Stuart-Fox, Martin. 1986. *Laos: Politics, Economics, and Society*. London: F. Pinter.

Tanter, Richard. 1990. "The Totalitarian Ambition: Intelligence Organisations in the Indonesian State." In *State and Civil Society in Indonesia*, edited by Arief Budiman, 213–88. Clayton: Centre of Southeast Asian Studies, Monash University.

Tedjasukmana, Iskandar. 1958. *The Political Character of the Indonesian Trade Union Movement*. Ithaca: Cornell University Modern Indonesia Project.

Tee, Kenneth. 2019. "MTUC Says Still Temporarily Suspended, Deregistration Still Possibl." *Malay Mail*, December 26, 2019. www.malaymail.com/news/malaysia/2019/12/26/mtuc-says-still-temporarily-suspended-deregistration-still-possible/1822407.

Tek, Farrah. 2022. "Making Law Matter: The Legal Mobilization of Subaltern Actors in Cambodia." Unpublished PhD dissertation. Minneapolis: University of Minnesota.

Than, Tin Maung Maung. 2007. *State Dominance in Myanmar: The Political Economy of Industrialization*. Singapore: Institute of Southeast Asian Studies.

Thompson, Mark R. 2021. "Pushback after Backsliding? Unconstrained Executive Aggrandizement in the Philippines versus Contested Military-Monarchical Rule in Thailand." *Democratization* 28 (1): 124–41.

Tjandra, Surya. 2016. "Labour Law and Development in Indonesia." Unpublished PhD thesis. Leiden: Leiden University.

Tjandraningsih, Indrasari. 2013. "State-Sponsored Precarious Work in Indonesia." *American Behavioral Scientist* 57 (4): 403–19. https://doi.org/10.1177/0002764212466236.

Tjandraningsih, Indrasari, and Hari Nugroho. 2008. "The Flexibility Regime and Organised Labour in Indonesia." *Labour and Management in Development* 9: 1–14.

Todd, Patricia, and Kwame Sundaram Jomo. 1988. "The Trade Union Movement in Peninsular Malaysia, 1957–1969." *Journal of Asian and African Studies* 23: 102–24.

Torres-Yu, Rosario. 2003. *Welgang Bayan: Empowering Labor Unions Against Poverty and Repression*. Manila: De La Salle University Press.

Tran, Angie Ngoc. 2007a. "The Third Sleeve: Emerging Labor Newspapers and the Response of the Labor Unions and the State to Workers' Resistance in Vietnam." *Labor Studies Journal* 32 (3): 257–79. https://doi.org/10.1177/0160449X07300716.

2007b. "Alternatives to the 'Race to the Bottom' in Vietnam: Minimum Wage Strikes and Their Aftermath." *Labor Studies Journal* 32 (4): 430–51. https://doi.org/10.1177/0160449X07300730.

2012. "Vietnamese Textile and Garment Industry in the Global Supply Chain: State Strategies and Workers' Responses." *Institutions and Economies* 4 (3): 123–50.

Tran, Angie Ngoc, Jennifer Bair, and Marion Werner. 2017. "Forcing Change from the Outside? The Role of Trade-Labour Linkages in Transforming Vietnam's Labour Regime." *Competition & Change* 21 (5): 397–416. https://doi.org/10.1177/1024529417729326.

Trocki, Carl A. 2001. "Development of Labor Organization in Singapore, 1800–1960." *Australian Journal of Politics and History* 47: 115–29.

Truong, Nhu. 2021. "Opposition Repertoires under Authoritarian Rule: Vietnam's 2016 Self-Nomination Movement." *Journal of East Asian Studies* 21 (1): 117–39. https://doi.org/10.1017/jea.2020.43.

Un, Kheang. 2019. *Cambodia: Return to Authoritarianism*. New York: Cambridge University Press. www.cambridge.org/core/elements/cambodia/6D6D419B9581E5204C34A5281AA76910.

Vogiatzoglou, Klimis. 2019. "Export Composition and Long-Run Economic Growth Impact: A Cointegration Analysis for ASEAN 'Latecomer' Economies." *Margin: The Journal of Applied Economic Research* 13 (2): 168–91. https://doi.org/10.1177/0973801018812571.

Wad, Peter. 2019. "Malaysian Trade Unions in the Twenty-First Century: Failed Revitalisation in a Market Economy." In *Trade Unions and Labour Movements in the Asia-Pacific Region*, edited by Byoung-Hoon Lee, Sek-Hong Ng, and Russell D. Lansbury, 166–84. New York: Routledge.

Ward, Kristy, and Vichhra Mouyly. 2016. "Employment Relations and Political Transition in Cambodia." *Journal of Industrial Relations* 58 (2): 258–72. https://doi.org/10.1177/0022185615620227.

Wehmhorner, Arnold. 1983. "Trade Unionism in Thailand – A New Dimension in a Modernizing Society." *Journal of Contemporary Asia* 13: 481–97.

Weiler, Peter. 1981. "The United States, International Labor, and the Cold War: The Breakup of the World Federation of Trade Unions." *Diplomatic History* 5 (1): 1–22. https://doi.org/10.1111/j.1467-7709.1981.tb00649.x.

Winters, Jeffrey. 2011. *Oligarchy*. New York: Cambridge University Press.

Worker Rights Consortium. 2014. "Crackdown in Cambodia: Workers SEeking Higher Wages Meet Repression." Washingon, DC: Worker Rights Consortium.

World Bank. 1976. "World Tables." Washington DC: The World Bank.

1978. "World Development Report, 1978." Washington DC: The World Bank.

1996. "From Plan to Market: World Development Report 1996." Washington, DC: The World Bank.

1997. "World Development Report 1997: The State in a Changing World." Washington DC: The World Bank.

Wurfel, David. 1959. "Trade Union Development and Labor Relations Policy in the Philippines." *Industrial & Labor Relations Review* 12: 582–608.

Cambridge Elements ☰

Politics and Society in Southeast Asia

Edward Aspinall

Australian National University

Edward Aspinall is a professor of politics at the Coral Bell School of Asia-Pacific Affairs, Australian National University. A specialist of Southeast Asia, especially Indonesia, much of his research has focused on democratisation, ethnic politics and civil society in Indonesia and, most recently, clientelism across Southeast Asia.

Meredith L. Weiss

University at Albany, SUNY

Meredith L. Weiss is Professor of Political Science at the University at Albany, SUNY. Her research addresses political mobilization and contention, the politics of identity and development, and electoral politics in Southeast Asia, with particular focus on Malaysia and Singapore.

About the Series

The Elements series Politics and Society in Southeast Asia includes both country-specific and thematic studies on one of the world's most dynamic regions. Each title, written by a leading scholar of that country or theme, combines a succinct, comprehensive, up-to-date overview of debates in the scholarly literature with original analysis and a clear argument.

Cambridge Elements ☰

Politics and Society in Southeast Asia

Elements in the Series

A full series listing is available at: www.cambridge.org/ESEA

Printed in the United States
by Baker & Taylor Publisher Services